Where to Eat SUSSEX

AN INFORMATIVE GUIDE TO EATING PLACES IN AND AROUND EAST AND WEST SUSSEX

Editor: Jeff Evans
Art and Design: Lyndsey Blackburn, Simon Baker
Editorial Assistant: Jackie Horne
Compilation: Mervyn Woodward, David Lemon

CONTENTS

Cover Photograph: Jack Fuller's, near Brightling, East Sussex
Back Cover Photograph: The Star Inn, Norman's Bay, Pevensey, East Sussex

Published by Kingsclere Publications Ltd.
Highfield House, 2 Highfield Avenue,
Newbury, Berkshire, RG14 5DS

Typeset by Wessex Press of Warminster Limited, Wiltshire
Produced through MRM Associates, Ltd., Reading, Berkshire

Distributed in the UK by AA Publishing,
The Automobile Association,
Fanum House, Basingstoke, Hampshire, RG21 2EA

Extreme care is taken to ensure the accuracy of entries, but
neither the Editor nor the Publishers accept any liability
for errors, omissions or other mistakes, or any
consequences arising therefrom.

ISBN 0 86204 186 4

Foreword

Mervyn Woodward

Foreword

BY MERVYN WOODWARD

The forewords for the many different *Where to Eat* guides are usually written by top chefs, hoteliers and restaurateurs. Sonia Stevenson, Franco Taruschio, Greta Hobbs, Nico Ladenis, Raymond Blanc, Jean-Yves Morel, Martin Skan, Ian MacAndrew, Francis Brennan and John Burton-Race are just a few of the famous people who have been kind enough to lend their names to, and bestow their commendations on, the *Where to Eat* series.

As compiler of four editions of the Kent guide, and co-compiler of four editions of the Sussex guide, I asked the publishers to allow me to write the foreword this year so that I could endorse public concern for safe food, cleanliness, freshness and hygiene. These have always been the factors uppermost in my mind when researching and preparing each edition. There is no substitute for quality, fresh produce, proper storage and preparation, and general attention to kitchen hygiene.

Furthermore, this is a good opportunity to state how I am continually surprised by the originality of the talented chefs, cooks and catering experts, many of them self-taught, whom I meet on my travels and who are included in *Where to Eat*. You, too, will surely discover this for yourselves.

To repeat, there is no substitute for quality, and this is what *Where to Eat in Sussex* is all about — this and value for money. I hope you find this guide useful in discovering new places, old favourites and the best food available. There's plenty of it about!

Mervyn Woodward
Co-Compiler

Tastes of SUSSEX

Sussex, at a first glance, seems to be an almost timeless county, with its prosperous country villages fringing their cricket greens, dominated by the parish church. But the county has always been influenced by the passing trends of its close neighbour, London, and its scenery stamped by successive waves of invaders. The once great forest of Anderida, which stretched from the county's northern border across the Weald to the edge of the Downs, was first cleared by Neolithic man and today it only remains in patches, such as Ashdown Forest. The Downs themselves, though still shrouded in the ancient mystique of their hilltop forts and prehistoric settlements, are no longer tended by shepherds and their flocks of

sheep in the pastoral scenes that inspired the painters Gainsborough and Fielding. And below the Downs lies a fertile coastal plain that was once an important foothold for potential invaders. The Romans left magnificent villas at Fishbourne and Bignor, the Saxons established

the Cinque Ports to ward off the Danes, and the Normans built imposing castles, such as the one at Arundel, to protect their conquest.

This variegated scenery has, over the centuries, produced a wealth of fresh produce, reflected in an unfussy style of home-cooking. There was never any need for Sussex cooks to mask the taste of inferior meat with heavy sauces, and, as if to emphasise the point, Downs' lamb tastes best when simply roasted in its own juices. Many of Sussex's traditional dishes are too heavy for modern tastes, for they evolved to satisfy the appetites of hungry yeomen farmers who worked long hours out in the fields. Suet is the common denominator, with the county's meat, fish, vegetables and fruit simply enveloped in a suet crust and steamed for a couple of hours. Acres Pudding was possibly the most basic, being a mixture of suet, raisins, flour and milk and so called because it could be eaten by the acre. Sussex Pond Pudding, on the other hand, has achieved fame

beyond the county boundary and was traditionally made with a whole unpeeled lemon, soaked in a surgary butter sauce and rolled up in a suet crust. Also popular, and much lighter to the palate, was Marigold Pudding which has a subtler flavour and is best served hot with thick cream.

cheese and ale, and supper was much the same. Meat was a luxury only to be enjoyed on a Sunday and in Sussex this would have been pork with Drip Pudding (made with suet which was boiled, sliced and then left in the dripping pan below the meat to absorb its juices), rather than roast beef with

Left-overs were never laid to waste. Spare suet balls would be boiled for about 20 minutes and then cut open and eaten hot with a dollop of butter and sugar, whilst pastry rounds would be baked into Coager Cakes as a mid-morning snack for farmworkers. These were similar to Plum Heavies which were also taken out into the fields and made by rubbing lard into flour, adding sugar, currants and soured milk, then rolling out the biscuits and baking them for about 15 minutes. Lunch usually consisted of bread,

Yorkshire Pudding.

Similarly, at Christmas pork was the traditional dish and not turkey. Pigs were always favoured because they were easy to keep, being fed on scraps, but they also had a special cultural significance which dated back to Saxon times when they roamed freely through the great forests. The highlight of the ancient year was the great Yule feast of December 21st, when Freya, the goddess of fertility, would ride across the sky on a chariot driven

by a boar and scatter the coming year's seeds. Gingerbread was also widely eaten at Christmas and, in Sussex, popular throughout the rest of the year as well. Yule Babies, in the image of Christ, were made out of gingerbread and at the great Horsham fairs, held five times a year, slabs would be shaped into famous personalities.

The numerous local fairs which were a welcome release from the routine of daily life have largely disappeared, but the village local, fulfilling a similar role, is still thriving. Today's homely, thatched inns, with their traditional beaming and polished horse-brasses, are a far cry from the sparsely furnished pubs of old. The pleasures of 'Sussex Swedes' (as the rural farmers were known) were simple, and their hostelries reflected this fact. Some modern inns similarly cater to the more sophisticated demands of the 20th century, providing one-arm

bandits and jukeboxes. Others have made determined efforts not to lose touch with their roots by displaying agricultural artefacts along their walls and offering wholesome, home-cooked food. The popularity of The Shepherd and Dog at Fulking, for example, stems from its collection of shepherds' crooks in the main bar and a stream which runs through the garden to the rear, in which the sheep were once washed before being taken to market. Some pubs still even play old inn games such as Murrells at The Blue Anchor, Portslade; Ringing the Bull at The Murrell Arms, Barnham, and Spinning Jenny at The Spotted Cow, Angmering. Likewise, the World Marble Championships, held once a year on the village green in front of The Greyhound at Tinsley Green, are always a big draw.

Today's pubs are certainly well-stocked with a wide range of drinks. Beer is supplied by both King and Barnes of Horsham, who

produce ales such as Sussex and Festive, and Harvey's of Lewes. Harvey's is a family-run business situated in an imposing Gothic brewery on the banks of the River Ouse, brewing a mild, a pale ale, a best bitter and the XXXX Old Ale. But, although beer remains the national drink, wine is fast growing in popularity and the Sussex countryside is dotted with a number of successful vineyards. Carr Taylor is one of the most widely established, producing over 100,000 bottles a year, the pioneer of a high wire trellis system which takes maximum advantage of the long daylight hours of the South of England. As yet there are no regional wines in Britain, but the

country as a whole is renowned for producing extremely dry vintages which take a long time to mature. Sussex is also a cider county, Merrydown being the fourth largest producer in the country. Furthermore, the English Farm Cider Centre is situated at Firle, stocking more than 100 varieties available for sale, or to be drunk direct from cask.

In the past, the cellars of most inns were supplemented by the illicit and highly profitable trade in smuggling. The whole of a village community, including even the local vicar, would either be involved directly or would turn a blind eye. Many pubs had secret passageways which have only recently come to light during renovation. At The Old House at Home, at Bosham Creek, there is a secret passage leading from behind one of the chimneys, whilst one of the walls of The Red Lion at Lindfield was knocked down to reveal a hoard of brandy and port. But probably the most famous of all the smuggling inns is The Star at Norman's Bay, Pevensey, which witnessed one of the bloodiest battles between smugglers and revenue men at the beginning of the 19th century, an event marking the decline of the smuggling trade.

Today the coastal pubs are

well-known for the quality and freshness of their fish dishes. Beachy Head prawns, Rye sole, Chichester eel, Arundel mullet and Selsey cockles, shrimps, crab and lobster number among favourite dishes, whilst Amberley is famed for its trout from the wild brooks. The reputation of Sussex fish attracted many illustrious personages, including the Prince Regent, later King George IV, who established Brighton as a fashionable resort. The prince was well known for his extravagance and gourmandising. One dish his chef, Marie-Antoine Careme, made famous was turbot à l'anglaise. The fish would be laid out on a silver platter, surrounded by alternating layers of black truffles and lobster flesh, with an outer border of creamed potatoes, and topped with pastry baskets containing pink roses made from lobster butter.

Sussex today draws a yearly influx of tourists and, intermingled with the busy seaside towns and isolated Downland villages, visitors will find numerous museums and working farms. Drusilla's at Alfriston has a restaurant serving Sussex foods, wines and ales, and also a bakery for take-away produce. There is a similar bakery, farm and tea shop at Bartley Mill, Yew Green, near Frant, which features a working watermill, and, at Buckley's Shop Museum in Battle, a Victorian arcade evocatively recreates the shopping habits of turn-of-the-century England. Most famous of all is the Weald and Downland Museum at Singleton which has rebuilt the buildings of ordinary countrymen on a 40 acre site and has working displays of rural crafts. Many of Sussex's agricultural traditions were withering under the onslaught of the 20th century. The fattiness of the Southdown sheep, for example, is no longer to modern tastes and the sheep have all but disappeared from the Downs. Museums such as The Weald and Downland are therefore important for keeping alive the old traditions, as well as providing an endless source of fascination and fun.

*Peckish
in Perth?*

*Hungry
in Holyhead?*

*Famished
in Felixstowe?*

*Ravenous
in Roscommon?*

WHERE
TO EAT

The discerning diner's guide
to restaurants throughout
Britain and Ireland

*Copies available from bookshops
or direct from the publishers*
Kingsclere Publications Ltd

YORK AND HUMBER

WHERE TO EAT
SURREY

WHERE TO EAT
GLOUCESTERSHIRE
THE COTSWOLDS
AND THE ROYAL FOREST OF DEAN

WHERE TO EAT
HAMPSHIRE

WHERE TO EAT
OXFORD
OXFORDSHIRE AND THE CHILTERNS

WHERE TO EAT
KENT

WHERE TO EAT
BERKSHIRE

WHERE TO EAT
DEVON & CORNWALL

WHERE TO EAT
SOMERSET

WHERE TO EAT
IRELAND

WHERE TO EAT
WALES

WHERE TO EAT
SCOTLAND

WHERE TO EAT
GUERNSEY
ALDERNEY, SARK AND HERM

Chef's Choice

In each of our regional **Where to Eat** *guides, we ask an experienced chef, well-respected in the area, to provide one of his favourite menus:*

Paul Hill

Paul Hill is owner/chef at the Waldernheath Country Restaurant in Hailsham. Having studied in Switzerland and in Paris, he opened the Waldernheath in 1969. Now, with his wife, Ann, and his two sons, he has established it as one of the most successful restaurants in the South.

STARTER

Crevettes Oscar

WINE

Rioja, Marques de Carceres 1985 or 1987

This recipe of prawns in a provençal sauce, topped with Stilton and garlic butter, served with French bread, is

adapted from a dish my wife and I enjoyed while on holiday on the island of Rhodes. It is quite rich and therefore needs a robust white or even red.

FISH COURSE

Coquilles St Jacques

WINE

Macon Fuissé 1988

Scallops, sautéed in butter rather than poached, are then covered with a light fish velouté with finely chopped mushrooms, topped with plenty of crunchy breadcrumbs and butter. Enough mashed potato is piped around to allow for plenty of sauce. A light white wine is the ideal accompaniment, such as that suggested.

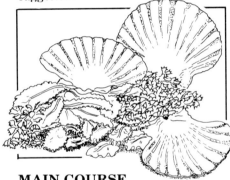

MAIN COURSE

Roast Gressingham Duck with Apricots and Damson Sauce

WINE

Côte Rotie, Bernard Burgaud 1986

These ducks can now be bought locally and are proving very popular. A cross between a mallard and a Norfolk duck, they are small but have a fine, slightly gamey flavour, without the fat of the Norfolk duck or the toughness sometimes found in the wild bird. We make our own damson cheese (a cross between jam and jelly) and use this to flavour the duck gravy and give it a lovely purple colour. Some apricot halves, soaked in brandy, are placed on the side.

DESSERT

Sussex Pond Pudding

WINE

Muscat de Beaumes de Venise or Barsac

Traditionally, this is made in a bowl lined with suet crust and filled with lemons, butter and Demerera sugar, steamed for two hours. We have adapted this recipe to include mixed fruit, which gives it more body and soaks up some of the juices. It's a very rich dessert, but wonderful when enjoyed occasionally, especially with a good, thick custard.

Introduction

This *Where to Eat* guide has been compiled to offer readers a good cross-section of eating places in the area. We do not only concentrate on the most expensive or the 'most highly rated' but endeavour to provide details of establishments which cater for all tastes, styles, budgets and occasions. Readers may discover restaurants (formal and informal), pubs, wine bars, coffee shops and tearooms and we thank proprietors and managers for providing the factual information.

We do not intend to compete with the established 'gourmet guides'. *Where to Eat* gives the facts — opening hours and average prices — combined with a brief description of the establishment. We do not use symbols or ratings. *Where to Eat* simply sets the scene and allows you to make the choice.

We state whether an establishment is open for lunch or dinner and prices quoted are for an à la carte three course meal or a table d'hôte menu, including service, as well as an indication of the lowest priced wine. However, whilst we believe these details are correct, it is suggested that readers check, when making a reservation, that prices and other facts quoted meet their requirements.

Two indexes are included at the back of the guide so that readers can easily pinpoint an establishment or a town or village. We always advise readers to use these indexes as, occasionally, late changes can result in establishments not appearing in a strictly logical sequence.

We hope that *Where to Eat* will provide you with the basis for many intimate dinners, special family occasions, successful business lunches or, perhaps, just an informal snack. A mention of this guide when you book may prove worthwhile. Let us know how things turned out. We are always pleased to hear from readers, be it praise, recommendations or criticism. Mark your envelopes for the attention of 'The Editor, Where to Eat Series'. Our address is:

Kingsclere Publications Ltd.
Highfield House, 2 Highfield Avenue,
Newbury, Berkshire. RG14 5DS.

We look forward to hearing from you. Don't forget, *Where to Eat* guides are now available for nearly every region of Britain, Ireland and the Channel Islands, each freshly researched and revised every year. If you're planning a holiday contact us for the relevant guide. Details are to be found within this book.

Where to Eat
SUSSEX

Mermaid Street, Rye

THE SHIP

South Harting.
Tel: (0703) 825302

Hours: *Open for coffee, lunch and dinner (last orders 9.30pm, 9pm Sun).*

Average Prices: *A la Carte £8–£10; Sun lunch £4.75; snacks £1.30.*

Wines: *House wine £5.25 per bottle.*

The cluster of Harting villages lie at the foot of hills on the Hampshire border. South Harting is easily the most distinctive, with its copper-clad church spire, and was for many years home to Trollope. The Ship Inn predates him by two centuries and has lost none of its original appeal with oak beams, fresh flowers, traditional ales (Ruddles) and wholesome cooking. The standard menu is supplemented by blackboard specials and features a selection of soups, pies, en croûte and flambé dishes, in addition to the customary range of pub fare and bar snacks. Popular individaul dishes include Selsey crab to start, followed by venison and beef pie, roast guinea fowl, pork normande or the unusual salmon flambé, with a traditional fruit crumble to complete. The emphasis is on the use of fresh local produce and even the chips are home-made. For a lighter snack, try one of the 'dinner jackets' (filled jacket potatoes) in the bar. Al fresco dining is possible in the small beer garden during mild weather.

THE SHIP

The Ship Inn South Harting

SOUTH HARTING. TEL: (0703) 825302

THE ELSTED INN

Elsted Marsh, Midhurst. Tel: (0730) 813662

Hours: *Open for coffee, lunch and dinner (last orders 10pm). Closed Sun evening.*

Average Prices: A la Carte £9; Sun lunch £3.95; snacks from £1.

Tweazle Jones, the new proprietress of The Elsted Inn, previously worked as an Egon Ronay inspector and has used that experience to good effect here. Simple English home-cooking is the order of the day, with a varied selection of pies, fresh fish, roasts and filling puddings. There is always a vegetarian dish on offer and many real ales and French regional wines to accompany.

THE BARLEYCORN

Main Road, Nutbourne. Tel: (0243) 573172

Hours: *Open for coffee, lunch and dinner (last orders 9.30pm).*

Average Prices: A la Carte £7; Sun lunch £5; snacks from 80p.

What sets apart this mid-17th century country pub is a macabre piece of recent history, for Ruth Ellis, her husband and lover all drank here on the night of the infamous murder. Run today by Linda and Alan Downey, it offers traditionally home-cooked food which extends from pepper steak, beef casserole or perhaps just a ploughman's for a main course, to apple crumble and spotted dick with custard for dessert. Real ales are available.

THE BARLEY MOW

Walderton, near Chichester. Tel: (0705) 631321

Hours: *Open for bar meals lunchtime and evening.*
Average Prices: A la Carte £6.70; Sun lunch £5.95; snacks from 90p.

On the edge of the deeply wooded South Downs, seven miles from Chichester, the 200-year-old Barley Mow is the friendly and attractive local for the village of Walderton. Its greenery won it a Perrier Floral Display

Clive & Julie Grace
The Barley Mow, Walderton
Nr. Chichester, PO18 9ED
(0705) 631321

Award in 1988 and its cooking always wins support. Popular dishes include steak and kidney pie, trout with almonds and sweet and sour pork, and there is always a selection of daily specials and filled jacket potatoes, as well as real ales.

All major credit cards accepted.

THE OLD HOUSE AT HOME

Cot Lane, Chidham. Tel: (0243) 572477
Hours: Open for lunch and dinner (last orders 10pm).
Average Prices: A la Carte £7; snacks from £1.20.

Chidham is a remote hamlet whose few houses cluster around the waters of Bosham creek. The Old House at Home has a centuries-old link with smuggling in the area. An interesting selection of real ales matches an equally extensive menu. Seven seafood dishes include fisherman's pie and there are over 15 meat and poultry dishes, with, for example, traditional chicken casserole. Snacks from the bar are numerous.

THE BELL INN

Bell Lane, Birdham, near Chichester. Tel: (0243) 512279

Hours: *Open for coffee, lunch, dinner and bar meals. No meals Sun evening in winter.*

Average Prices: *A la Carte £10; Sun lunch £6; snacks from £1.95.*

The popular Bell Inn, built in 1950, stands on the Bracklesham Bay road from Chichester. Its L-shaped bar has a restaurant area at one end and here traditional dishes such as whole local plaice served on the bone, steaks, and escalope of veal with ham and cheese are offered. There are speciality jacket potatoes, daily specials and real ales.

The Bell Inn

Bell Lane, Birdham Nr. Chichester, Sussex
Tel: Birdham 512279

WHITE SWAN

STATION ROAD, BOSHAM, Nr. CHICHESTER ☎ 0243 573381

17

THE CRAB AND LOBSTER

Mill Lane, Sidlesham. Tel: (0243) 56233

Hours: *Open for lunch and dinner (last orders 9.30pm). Closed Tues.*

Average Prices: *Snacks from £2.90; house wine £5.40 per bottle.*

The Crab and Lobster is a pub whose character has not suffered from refurbishment plans. It sits overlooking the 1,000 acre maritime nature reserve of Pagham Harbour and is traditional also in its ales and menus. The inevitable fresh crab and lobster are available, along with the more unusual chicken satay and the favourite steak and kidney pie. Pineapple ginger cheesecake or treacle tart make satisfying conclusions.

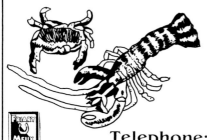

The Crab & Lobster,
Mill Lane,
Sidlesham,
Chichester,
West Sussex PO20 7NB

Telephone: Sidlesham (0243 56) 233

THE WHEATSHEAF INN

Rumbolds Hill, Midhurst. Tel: (073 081) 3450

Hours: *Open for lunch and dinner.*

Average Prices: *A la Carte £10; snacks from £1.50.*

Run by Brian and Elaine Simpson, The Wheatsheaf is situated in central Midhurst. Dating back to 1630, its age and character are revealed in a wealth of beaming and brass. The basic pub menu features a range of steaks, pies, pizzas and quiches, but the speciality of the house is fresh crab and lobster direct from Selsey. A courtyard garden beckons in fine weather and real ales are on draught.

The Wheatsheaf Inn

Brian & Elaine
Simpson
Mid 3450

Rumbolds Hill, Midhurst, W. Sussex

THE RICHARD COBDEN INN

Cocking, near Midhurst. Tel:(073 081) 2974

Hours:　　　　*Open for coffee, lunch (except Mon) and dinner. No meals Sun evening in winter.*

Average Prices: A la Carte from £9; wine from £4.75; snacks £1.20.

Named in honour of the famous popular agitator, Richard Cobden, who helped with the repeal campaign against the infamous Victorian Corn Laws, this inn is situated on the A286 Midhurst–Chichester road. Today the emphasis is traditional, not radical, and a regularly-changing blackboard menu of pub favourites is served. T-bone and peppered steaks and vegetarian dishes are always available. Garden at the rear.

The Richard Cobden Inn
Free House

Cocking, Nr. Midhurst, West Sussex
Telephone: Midhurst (0730) 812974

THE WHITE HORSE

Graffham, near Petworth. Tel: (079 86) 331

Hours:　　　　*Open for lunch and dinner.*

Average Prices: A la Carte £8; Sun lunch from £3.95.

The White Horse, run by Les and Jenny Hellier, is situated in delightful countryside on the north side of the South Downs. A wide range of real ales is offered in the comfortable bar. The small restaurant area is non-smoking for the comfort of diners and offers home-cooked special meals and a full menu and bar snacks. The well-furnished rear garden is ideal for families. Reservations are recommended, especially for Sunday roast lunches.

The White Horse

GRAFFHAM
WEST SUSSEX GU28 0NT
Telephone: Graffham 331

19

THE TRUNDLE INN

West Dean, near Chichester.
Tel: (024 363) 246

Hours: *Open for lunch and dinner. Closed Sun evening and Mon.*

Average Prices: *A la Carte £10; Sun lunch £5.95; snacks from £2.*

Wines: *House wine £4.85 per bottle.*

For racing enthusiasts there couldn't be a more appropriate place to eat than at The Trundle Inn. Named after the nearby 700ft hillock, with its sweeping views out over the Downs and Goodwood racecourse, the racing theme predominates in Colours Restaurant. One of the owners, Fred Dunning, formerly worked for a West Country trainer and he has displayed on the walls what is believed to be the largest pub collection of racing memorabilia. The amusing menu adopts the same theme. Main course dishes include steak, charcoal-grills, fish, ribs of lamb and roast Sussex suckling pig, whilst 'at the final furlong' customers can select their dessert from the sweet trolley. For those who make it to 'the finish', there is a selection of fine ports and champagne brandy. The restaurant is particularly convenient for visitors to West Dean College, which offers residential courses in country crafts. Private parties are catered for and all major credit cards are welcomed. The Trundle is situated situated on the A286 Chichester–Midhurst road and has ample car parking.

THE ROYAL OAK

Pook Lane, East Lavant.
Tel: (0243) 527434

Hours:	*Open for coffee, lunch and dinner (last orders 10pm). Closed Sun/Mon evenings.*
Average Prices:	*A la Carte £10; snacks from £2.50.*
Wines:	*House wine £5.95 per bottle.*

Mid and East Lavant, despite their proximity to Chichester, have remained characterful little villages untouched by encroaching suburbia. The Royal Oak was built during the 1760's and conspicuous efforts have been made to ensure that it remains in the country tradition of oak beaming and flagstoned flooring, with not a fruit machine or jukebox in sight. Real ales (Friary Meux and King and Barnes) are served and the daily menu is chalked up on the blackboard. Lunchtime fare includes dishes such as smoked turkey breast and avocado, Sussex crock pot, oak-smoked ribs and celery and Stilton pie. During the summer months, meals can be enjoyed in the cottage garden. In the evening, steak and Guinness pie, fresh lemon sole or a mixed seafood platter might be preceded by gravad lax, home-made pâté or a half-pint of prawns, with home-made treacle tart to conclude. The pub is a popular haunt for racegoers from Goodwood and theatregoers from Chichester.

EARL OF MARCH

Lavant Road, Lavant, Chichester. Tel: (0243) 774751

Hours: *Open for lunch and dinner.*

Average Prices: *A la Carte £6; snacks from 70p.*

A selection of no less than 21 draught beers are served at this pub which enjoys a fine reputation for its home-cooked food. The cosy, neat dining area is clustered around a large fireplace and the promptly served dishes include game (venison, hare and pheasant) or perhaps chicken en croûte, as well as the traditional inn favourites like ploughman's, cottage pie and chilli. The garden, dominated by the surrounding downland, is a pleasant place to eat or drink during the summer months.

THE MURRELL ARMS

Yapton Road, Barnham. Tel: (0243) 553320

Hours: *Open for bar meals lunchtimes and evenings.*

Average Prices: *Bar meals £1–£4.*

The Murrel Arms is very much a village pub in the old sense, overlooking the green and involved in all aspects of village life. The ancient game of ringing the bull is still played at the pub, antique auctions take place every alternate Wednesday and, once a year, on 4th August, a sheep roast is held. Real ales, country wines and bar meals are served in each of its three bars. The speciality is bacon hock with a parsley sauce.

THE HORSE AND GROOM

Singleton, near Chichester.
Tel: (024 363) 282

Hours: *Open for coffee, lunch, tea and dinner.*
Average Prices: *A la Carte £9; Sun lunch £6.50; snacks from £2.50.*
Wines: *House wine £3.50 per bottle.*

The roadside Horse and Groom has undergone many improvements since Tim and Lynne Jones took over and has remained popular with local villagers, whilst attracting visitors with its reputation for good food. The proprietors' emphasis on freshness in their cooking even extends to importing bread direct from France each day for use in the 'ploughperson's' lunch. There is a separate restaurant area which is served by two wide-ranging blackboard menus, one of which changes daily. Longstanding pub favourites such as home-made soups, steak and kidney pie in ale, steak Diane and chicken Kiev all appear and the home-cooked ham is considered something of a house speciality. The highlights of the summer months are cream teas and barbecues, both of which can be enjoyed in the large garden. The pub is particularly popular with visitors to the nearby Weald and Downland Open Air Museum which has reconstructed a variety of historical buildings and provides demonstrations of rural crafts.

Goodwood Park Hotel
Golf & Country Club

Goodwood, Chichester, West Sussex PO18 0QB
Tel: (0243) 775537 · Telex: 869173 GPKHTL · Fax: (0243) 533802

THE DUKE'S RESTAURANT AT THE GOODWOOD PARK HOTEL

Goodwood, near Chichester.
Tel: (0243) 775537

Hours: *Open for coffee, lunch, tea and dinner.*

Average Prices: *A la Carte £15–£20; Table d'Hôte lunch £11.50;*
                        Sun lunch £12.50.

Wines: *House wine £8 (white), £9 (red) per bottle.*

Goodwood Park, the ancestral home of the Dukes of Richmond, has always moved with the times. Over the years the estate has progressively opened itself up to the public with its horse racing, aerodrome, motor circuit, and golf courses. The distinctive mansion, with its Doric columned entrance designed by Wyatt, is also open to the public.

At the gateway to the estate stands a 17th century coaching inn, once known as The Richmond Arms. After a multi-million pound investment by Goodwood and Country Club Hotels, it has now been transformed into a luxury 90-bedroomed hotel, particularly geared to the business trade.

The Duke's Restaurant still has very much of the atmosphere of a traditional hostelry, with its whitewashed walls and heavy tie-beaming running across the room. Against this setting a predominantly French menu is served.

Starters feature a soup, a terrine or perhaps a parfait of smoked salmon with local lobster, whilst the main course is split into three sections. The first, 'From River and Sea', details fish dishes such as grilled fillet of turbot (with a lobster butter sauce and fresh lime) and supreme of wild Scottish salmon (baked in filo pastry with crabmeat and served with a creamy tomato sauce infused with ginger and fennel). Secondly, there is 'From Farm and Forest' with, for example, sauté of free-range chicken (cooked with Sauternes and Riesling wines, smoked bacon and truffles, finished with cream), and medallions of Sussex venison with a grand veneur sauce. For vegetarians there are guaranteed-no-meat tagliolini — 'meat balls' in an Italian sauce with grated Pecorino cheese. Concluding are home-made desserts, sorbets, a cheeseboard and coffee with sweetmeats.

At lunch and dinner time there is a set menu with a choice of four courses including pink trout, Aberdeen Angus beef, Sussex chicken and pot-roasted partridge. Residents and club members also have the option of eating in the Waterbeach Grill and Bar which overlooks the swimming pool.

INGLENOOK HOTEL AND RESTAURANT

255 Pagham Road, Nyetimber, Bognor Regis.
Tel: (0243) 262495

Hours:　　　　　*Open for coffee, lunch, tea and dinner.*
Average Prices:　A la Carte £12–£15; Sun lunch £8.50; snacks £2.50.

Three miles from Bognor Regis and on the doorstep of the Pagham Nature Reserve, The Inglenook Hotel has all the appeal of a country cottage, with its whitewashed walls and colourful flowerboxes on the outside and comfy furnishings within. The atmosphere of its 16th century origins is preserved by the beaming which criss-crosses the ceilings of many of the rooms. The restaurant is also imbued with a refined country atmosphere, blending oak furnishings with pink napery and fresh flowers. The menu itself is traditionally orientated with, for example, rollmop herrings in mustard and Jamaican grapefruit amongst the starters. Fresh local fish is well to the fore on the list of main course dishes, alongside lobster, crab and meat and poultry dishes such as duck anglaise and entrecôte steak. Lighter snacks can be taken in the bar or, weather permitting, outside in the garden. Open sandwiches are a speciality. Real ales are on draught and all major credit cards are accepted.

Inglenook

Sixteenth Century
Hotel and
Fully Licensed
Restaurant

255 Pagham Road, Nyetimber,
Bognor Regis, West Sussex,
England PO21 3QB
Telephone: Pagham 0243 262495

It is not our intention to compete with the established 'gourmet guides'. We aim to set the scene and let you, the reader, make the choice. However, we are always pleased to hear from both readers and advertisers, be it praise, recommendations or criticism.

COSTELLOS RESTAURANT

Felpham Village, near Bognor Regis.
Tel: (0243) 866124

Hours: *Open for dinner, except Sun/Mon. Lunch on Sun and tea in summer.*

Average Prices: *Table d'Hôte £9.95; Sun lunch £6.95.*

One minute from the beach and just five minutes' drive from Bognor, two former Royal Navy officers, Paul and Karen King, have launched their own restaurant. Costellos, decorated in contrasting mint green

and monarch red, has attractive lattice screens to separate the tables and give a more private air. Karen's 'galley' presents a range of appetising dishes such as supreme of chicken with a creamy asparagus sauce and Selsey crab au gratin (on a scallop shell, piped with dauphinoise potato, topped with grated cheese). 24 wines include an 'own label' house wine.

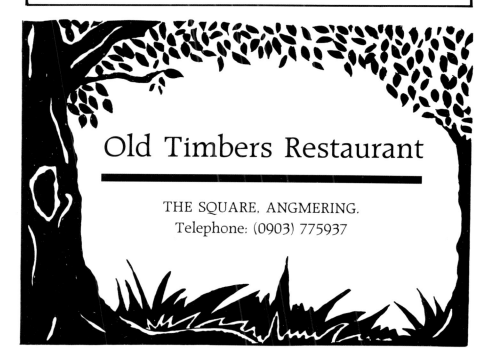

Old Timbers Restaurant

THE SQUARE, ANGMERING.
Telephone: (0903) 775937

the pasta place

49 Aldwich Road, Bognor Regis.
Tel: (0243) 865555

Hours: Open from 12 noon for coffee, lunch, tea and dinner (last orders 11.30pm).

Average Prices: A la Carte £8.50; single course specials £2.25.

Wines: House wine £4.95 per bottle.

To downtown Bognor Regis Nick and Barbara Foxcroft have brought a refreshingly different attitude to catering, with their smart Italian chic. Black bent wood chairs contrast marble topped tables and contemporary prints which frame the walls. The pasta itself is made daily on the premises in six styles, accompanied by a list of sauces. These include pescatore (a fish sauce with clams, mussels, prawns, squid, tomatoes and garlic) and giardino (courgettes and broccoli tossed in butter and garlic, with tomatoes, onions and herbs). The pizzas are also very popular, especially the 'Godfather' which is claimed to be "the pizza you can't refuse". In all, the menu lists over 40 starters, main courses and vegetarian dishes, all supplemented by a daily specials board which adds even more variety. To conclude there is a wide range of desserts and Italian ice creams. All the major credit cards are accepted and the restaurant can be found close to the sea.

ANCTON HOUSE HOTEL AND RESTAURANT

Ancton Lane, Middleton-on-Sea.
Tel: (024 369) 2482

Hours:	*Open for coffee, lunch, tea and dinner. Closed Mon/Tues evenings. Bar meals, except Sun lunch.*
Average Prices:	*Table d'Hôte £13.95; Sun lunch £6.95.*
Wines:	*House wine £4.50 per bottle.*

16th century Ancton House is very much a farmhouse home. Set close to the shore and overlooking the Arun Valley, it has a relaxing and old-fashioned ambience that is immediately appealing to those seeking the peace of the countryside. Rooms are unpretentiously decorated, produce comes fresh from the hotel's own gardens and the atmosphere under the new proprietors, Susan and Allan English, is welcoming. Fish is a speciality of the menu with bouillabaisse for starter and dishes such as salmon in filo pastry, bass with fennel and fillet of sole nantaise (lobster sauce) for the main course. Meat dishes include poussin au Romarin (spring chicken grilled with herbs), tournedos Rossini (served on a croûton and garnished with pâté de foie and a Madeira sauce) and suprême de canard à l'orange (breast of duck cooked with orange, curaçao and an orange sauce). The accompanying wine list is select and its highlight a German label exclusively from Rheinpfalz. There is also a small cocktail bar attached to the restaurant.

BAILIFFSCOURT HOTEL AND RESTAURANT

Climping, Littlehampton.
Tel: (0903) 723511   Fax: (0903) 723107

Hours: *Open for breakfast, coffee, lunch, tea and dinner (last orders 9.45pm).*

Average Prices: *A la Carte £27; Table d'Hôte £19.50; lunch £15.50; summer buffet from £11.95,*

Wines: *House wine £9.50 per bottle; £1.75 per glass.*

"An exclusive hotel of extraordinary beauty and fascination" has been one description given to Bailiffscourt. Although it was built by Lord Moyne in the late 1920's, it is an atmospheric re-creation of a Medieval manor, set within 23 acres of tranquil parkland. Here new chef, Jonas Tester, presents an imaginative menu of dishes from fresh seasonal ingredients. From late spring to early autumn, Bailiffscourt is well known for its summer buffet which can be taken in the rose-clad courtyard. It offers a wide-ranging choice which may include fresh Selsey lobster poached in Noilly Prat and dill, served chilled with salads and home-made mayonnaise. Every Saturday a gourmet menu is served, becoming the regular à la carte selection for the rest of the week. Dishes here have featured supreme of chicken Jack Daniels (breast braised in consomme and served in a cream sauce laced with Jack Daniels Tennessee Mash and garnished with a julienne of celery), and fricassée of rabbit and leeks.

Discover the magic of

Bailiffscourt

CLIMPING, WEST SUSSEX
Enquiries or Reservations:
LITTLEHAMPTON (0903) 723511

THE BLACK RABBIT

Mill Lane, Offam, Arundel. Tel: (0903) 882828

Hours:	*Open for dinner. Bar meals lunchtimes daily and evenings weekend.*
Average Prices:	*A la Carte £10–£12; Sun lunch £4.50 (1 course).*
Wines:	*House wine £5.95 per bottle.*

The Black Rabbit has what can only be described as an idyllic location, one, in fact, that inspired both Constable and Turner. The inn lies on the banks of the River Arun, overlooking the imposing castle which dominates all around it. Making the most of its situation, The Black Rabbit has waterside seating and large windows looking out from the bar. It is a popular venue for lunchtime bar snacks and has a blackboard displaying the daily specials in the carvery service area, where there is also a help-yourself salad bar. Typical of the choice might be Hungarian goulash, lasagne, a seafood platter or, more simply, jumbo sausages. The large restaurant serves only in the evenings and has an internationally-orientated menu which opens with starters such as calamari or crudités with dips. Main course dishes include Hawaiian chicken, steak on a stick and sizzling fajitas (piping hot chicken or steak on sizzling skewers with peppers and onions). There is an accompanying list of about 25 popular European and Californian wines and all major credit cards are accepted.

The Black Rabbit

Mill Lane, Offham, Arundel, West Sussex

TEL: (0903) 882828

31

QUINS RESTAURANT

Houghton Bridge, near Amberley.
Tel: (0798) 831790

Hours: *Open for lunch and dinner.*

Average Prices: *A la Carte £15–£20; Sun lunch £12.50; Table d'Hôte lunch £7.50.*

Wines: *House wine £5.90 per bottle.*

The patio terrace at Quins Restaurant is a peaceful and engaging setting in which to enjoy a leisurely meal overlooking Houghton Bridge and the River Arun flowing beneath. Brothers Peter and Paul Dixon have recently acquired the premises and crafted a menu which perfectly accords with the restaurant's air of country sophistication. Appetisers are light. A half-melon filled with a pear granite and garnished with fresh seasonal fruits, or pastry mirabelle (puff pastry pillow filled with mushroom, smoked bacon and spinach) whets the appetite for the main course. Here there are about eight dishes to choose from, with Dover sole, turbot, veal, steak and poultry dishes such as fanned supreme of magret duckling (grilled pink and served with an apple and mint compote). All dishes are served with rösti potato (a Swiss speciality), market fresh vegetables or side salad. The luncheon menu does not stint on quality and has proved particularly popular, offering dishes like steamed escalope of salmon (placed on a bed of leeks cordoned with a chive butter sauce).

QUINS RESTAURANT

HOUGHTON BRIDGE · AMBERLEY · Nr ARUNDEL
WEST SUSSEX

TELEPHONE (0798) 831790

THE SWAN HOTEL

High Street, Arundel. Tel: (0903) 882314

Hours: *Open for coffee, lunch, tea and dinner (last orders 9.30pm).*

Average Prices: *A la Carte £11.50; Table d'Hôte £9; Sun lunch £7; snacks from £2.*

Wines: *House wine £6 per litre.*

Many of Arundel's houses mirror the surrounding monuments through their air of antiquity and this is nowhere more evident than at The Swan Hotel. Situated close to the river, its aim is to provide a comfortable and welcoming setting, with traditional and wholesome food to match. To this end, the wholemeal bread is locally-baked, the butcher calls daily and fish is drawn locally, guaranteeing both freshness and quality. Appetisers include Swiss chicken salad, and smoked salmon with crab mousse. Among the most popular main course dishes are seafood pie, rack of lamb with a honey and rosemary sauce, breast of duck in a black cherry sauce with brandy and chicken Swan Lake (breast of chicken filled with cream cheese, prawns and oregano, served with a cream sauce with cucumber). As a finishing touch there is a wide choice of teas and liqueur coffees. Bar meals include chilli, ploughman's lunches and Barnsley chops. Live music every Sunday. Major credit cards are welcomed.

The Swan Hotel

High Street, Arundel. Tel: (0903) 882314

POGEY'S

25 Tarrant Street, Arundel. Tel: (0903) 882222
Hours: *Open for lunch and dinner.*
Average Prices: A la Carte £10–£15; Sun lunch £6.95.

Pogey's is a colourfully decorated, 20's-style restaurant, with a 200-year-old grapevine to add character and a spacious cocktail bar for pre-dinner drinks. The menu covers appetising dishes such as poached chicken supreme with an old English mead sauce, roast magret duck with a piquant raspberry sauce and, for vegetarians, mushroom and pasta crunch.

POGEY'S RESTAURANT,

25 TARRANT STREET,
ARUNDEL, W. SUSSEX

☎ ARUNDEL 882222

THIRTIES

25a Tarrant Street, Arundel. Tel: (0903) 884414
Hours: *Open for lunch and dinner.*
Average Prices: Bar meals from £2.95.

Thirties is a characterful wine bar/bistro situated on the ground floor below Pogey's. Its popular menu and wine and cocktail selections are blackboard-listed, changing daily. For al fresco dining during the summer months there is an attractive patioed garden which features a giant-sized chess set. Pogey's and Thirties are conveniently and centrally located.

THIRTIES WINE & COCKTAIL BAR

25A TARRANT STREET, ARUNDEL, WEST SUSSEX
☎ ARUNDEL (0903) 884414

THE GEORGE AND DRAGON INN

Burpham, Arundel. Tel: (0903) 883131

Hours:	*Open for lunch, dinner daily, except Sun (last orders 9.30pm). Bar meals.*
Average Prices:	*Prix fixé £20.35; Sun lunch £11; snacks from £1.35.*
Wines:	*House wine £6.50 per bottle.*

Burpham is one of the many Downland villages which lie along the water-meadows of the River Arun as it traces its path down to the sea. The village is distinguished by imposing earthworks, once an ancient fort that protected the whole Arun Valley. Today they lie in the shadow of the village's Norman church and close to The George and Dragon.

The pub has a trim Georgian front and a newly refurbished interior. Ian and Janet Wilson, the proprietors, have transformed its reputation and food is now a major attraction. There is a separate restaurant (seating 24), under the guidance of chef Michael Collis, who designs all his own menus and is a believer in freshly cooked food. The main dinner menu is, therefore, seasonally based.

There is usually a choice of about seven starters, including such appetisers as smoked duck breast with lychee, pancake blinis of seafood and spinach under a cheese sauce, and breast of wood pigeon (sautéed in butter with a hint of red wine). The main course intermingles seasonal game and fish, with dishes such as sole fillets in filo pastry with a Choron sauce; quail, boned and stuffed with wild mushrooms and rice, and Scotch sirloin steak served with a delicate watercress and garlic sauce. Wines are mainly French but with a scattering of some from other European countries. To conclude there is a wide selection of cheeses or home-made desserts like cheesecake topped with peaches and fresh kiwi fruit.

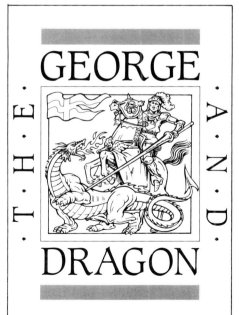

Ian Wilson takes a keen interest in real ales and this is reflected in the bar. A selection of snacks is also served here, both from a regular menu and a blackboard where daily specials are chalked. Sandwiches, steaks, gammon, fish and jacket potatoes are all served. The choice of ploughman's lunches involves a 'Forester' (pâté and cucumber) and an 'Olde England' (Stilton and apple).

HOWARDS

HOTEL AND RESTAURANTS
☎ **Arundel (0903) 882655**

Crossbush, Arundel.
Tel: (0903) 882655   Fax: (0903) 883384

Hours:	*Carvery open lunchtime and evening. Café des Amis open Tues–Sat evenings (last orders 10pm).*
Average Prices:	*Carvery £8.95; six course meal £12.50.*
Wines:	*House wine £6 per bottle.*

Howards Hotel which opened in 1984 is situated on the A27 which runs south to Worthing. It offers the diner a choice of three venues; a traditional carvery/restaurant, the hotel bar and the more informal

Café des Amis. The daily carvery in the restaurant has roast meats, fresh local fish and prime steaks for its main course selection, followed by a selection of sweets or cheeses. All main courses are served with a selection of fresh vegetables. The Café des Amis, on the other hand, is decorated with colourful murals of French street scenes and serves bistro-style cooking. Meals begin with crudites, dips, pâté or mousse and crusty French bread, and continue with a choice of starters and main courses. The whole menu consists of traditional French dishes, with the emphasis on seafood and fish, then there is a choice from the extensive cheeseboard, followed by fruit pastries and finally coffee.

CAFE DES AMIS

THE SPUR

Slindon, near Arundel.
Tel: (024 365) 216

Hours: *Open for lunch and dinner.*
Average Prices: *A la Carte £11; carvery £7.50 (three courses).*
Wines: *House wine £6.50 per bottle.*

Slindon is a showpiece 17th century village lying at the heart of 3,000 acres of National Trust woodland. Despite hurricane damage to the beechwoods, the area still attracts many walkers who use the village as a base for walks westwards along the downs and visits to the old Roman road, Stane Street. The whitewashed walls of The Spur and its jumble of plant boxes present an enticing frontage, whilst new chefs José and Marie Biejas (formerly of The White Horse, Chilgrove) attract customers even more with their style of home-cooking. Dishes like chicken cordon bleu, scampi Spur-style and Portuguese sardines can be found in the restaurant's à la carte selection and there is also a separate carvery/charcoal-grill. In the bar snacks are chalked up on a blackboard and these can also be taken into the garden. Private parties are catered for and accommodation is also provided. The village itself can be found about half a mile off the A29 Chichester–Pulborough road.

The village pond at Lindfield.

THE HALF MOON INN

Northchapel, near Petworth. Tel: (042 878) 270

Hours: *Open for coffee, lunch and dinner.*

Average Prices: *A la Carte £10; Sun lunch £7.50; snacks £1.50.*

Situated on the A283 Petworth–Guildford road, The Half Moon is a traditional country inn dating back to the 15th century with oak beaming, a warm inglenook fire and many agricultural artefacts along the walls. There is an extensive blackboard-displayed menu with dishes such as home-made steak and kidney pie and Northchapel savoury sausages. Ample car parking.

THE ANGEL HOTEL AND CARVERY

Angel Street, Petworth. Tel: (0798) 42153

Hours: *Open for coffee, lunch and dinner. No carvery Sun/Mon/Tues. Bar meals lunchtime.*

Average Prices: *Carvery lunch £4.50 (1 course); dinner £6.95.*

Under the Pellant family, The Angel has become a thriving hotel. Its popular carvery seats over 60 guests and features a joint of the day and daily-changing specials. Traditional desserts (such as home-made treacle tart) are favourites to conclude. The refurbished bar area serves real ales and a selection of hearty snacks, all to be enjoyed in the garden during the summer.

THE WELLDIGGERS ARMS

Pulborough Road, Petworth.
Tel: (0798) 42287

Hours:	*Open for lunch and dinner. Bar meals.*
Average Prices:	*A la Carte £10–£12; snacks from £1.50.*
Wines:	*House wine £7 per litre; £1 per glass.*

The Welldiggers Arms can be found on the main A283
Petworth–Pulborough road. Run by Ted and Pat Whitcomb, it is a
traditional 300-year-old inn with the essential accompaniments of an
inglenook fireplace, a country setting overlooking downland and a
selection of real ales on draught (Truman's, Tamplin's and Young's). The
Welldiggers is also well known locally for its cooking, specialising in
seafood, local game and prime steaks, according to seasonal availability.
Try fresh asparagus, grilled sardines or salad niçoise as a starter, followed
by a main course from fresh salmon, roast duck, oxtail casserole and
more. Typical of the game selection might be pheasant, partridge or
grouse, and for vegetarians courgette cheesebake is one option. Lighter
bar meals are also available and these include jumbo prawns, whitebait
and pâté. Accompanying wines are carefully selected with an emphasis on
Burgundies. With all the major credit cards accepted, The Welldiggers
makes a good watering hole for visitors to local sights such as Petworth
House.

THE WELLDIGGERS ARMS
PETWORTH 42287
FAMOUS FOR FOOD

TUDOR COTTAGE RESTAURANT

Saddlers Row, Petworth. Tel: (0798) 42125

Hours: *Open for coffee, lunch, tea and dinner.*
Average Prices: *A la Carte £7.50 (dinner), £5.70 (lunch).*

Hospitality and atmosphere are just two attributes of the 15th century Tudor Cottage which also has an array of home produce for sale, including preserves and freshly-roasted coffee. The restaurant (which has been open for around 100 years) features casseroles, pies, fondues and unusual dishes such as chicken and broccoli lasagne, with vegetarians well looked after. Steamed pudding or fruit crumble is available to finish, with a remarkable choice between 11 set teas during the day (one for children).

Tudor Cottage Restaurant

Saddlers Row
Petworth West Sussex
Petworth 42125

Proprietors Brian and Sue Barnhurst

THE LION'S DEN AT THE RED LION

New Street, Petworth. Tel: (0798) 42181

Hours: *Open for lunch and evening meals (last orders 9.30pm).*
Average Prices: *A la Carte £10.50; Sun lunch £4.50; snacks £1.50.*

A 400-year-old listed building with open fire and a cobbled courtyard for summer drinking sets the scene at The Red Lion. Family-run, it is also noted for its wholesome home-cooking and friendly relaxed atmosphere. Soup of the day could be followed by steak and mushroom pie or chilli con carne, with chocolate fudge cake to finish. Fremlins and Flowers Original real ales are on draught.

The Red Lion

NEW STREET, PETWORTH, SUSSEX.
Telephone: (0798) 42181.

THE HALF MOON

Kirdford, near Billingshurst. Tel: (040 377) 223

Hours: Open for lunch and dinner (last orders 9.30pm). Closed Sun evening/Mon.

Average Prices: A la Carte £6.50; Sun lunch £5.95; snacks 95p.

The Half Moon was built by knocking three cottages into one and has a quarry tiled floor in the public bar. Bar snacks are wide-ranging and include vegetarian dishes. Daily specials, jacket potatoes, steaks and fish dishes (such as plaice Kiev) are all popular. There is a large equipped play garden for children.

THE THREE CROWNS

Wisborough Green. Tel: (0403) 700207

Hours: Open for coffee, lunch and dinner.

Average Prices: A la Carte £8; snacks from 90p.

At The Three Crowns, proprietors Brian and Sandy Yeo offer a menu with filling country portions. Sandwiches, ploughman's lunches, salads, omelettes, pizzas and other platters sit side by side with home-cooked steak and kidney pie and Madras chicken curry. Traditional sponge desserts are a finishing treat. Booking is advisable. Real ales are on draught in the bar.

THE BAT AND BALL

Newbund Lane, Wisborough Green. Tel: (0403) 700313
Hours: *Open for lunch and dinner. Closed Mon evenings.*
Average Prices: *A la Carte £8–£10; Sun lunch £6.50; snacks £1.20.*

Standing opposite the village's former cricket pitch, The Bat and Ball is an old pub with a wealth of beams and is a lovely spot for a relaxing drink in the country. Traditional bar meals are provided and include cottage pie, spaghetti bolognaise, omelettes, ploughman's lunches, sandwiches, burgers and basket meals. Morris dancers entertain once a month.

THE BAT AND BALL
WISBOROUGH GREEN
TEL: (0403) 700313

NEWSTEAD HALL HOTEL

Adversane, Billingshurst. Tel: (040 381) 3196
Hours: *Open for dinner and Sun lunch.*
Average Prices: *A la Carte £10–£15; Sun lunch from £7.*

Comfortable furnishings set against oak panelling place Newstead Hall in the time-honoured tradition of old-style family-run hotels. This is also reflected in the British emphasis of its restaurant menu which presents dishes such as pork piquant (with a spicy tomato sauce), trout with cucumber, and lamb chop with rosemary in a wild blackberry sauce. Pleasant grounds. Two miles south of Billingshurst on the A29.

𝔑𝔢𝔴𝔰𝔱𝔢𝔞𝔡 𝔥𝔞𝔩𝔩 HOTEL

TELEPHONE BILLINGSHURST 3196

GROOMSLAND HOUSE RESTAURANT

Parbrook, Billingshurst.
Tel: (0403) 782571

Hours: *Open for lunch and dinner (last orders 10pm).*
                Closed Mon.

Average Prices: *A la Carte £14; Sun lunch £9.50; snacks from £1.95.*
Wines: *House wine £5.25 per bottle.*

The village of Billingshurst can be found on the A29 London–Pulborough road. Groomsland House is situated to the south of the village and has two rooms available for overnight accommodation. It is best known, however, for its 15th century restaurant. Exposed beams, open log fires during the winter months and cosily set tables accompany a traditional Anglo-French menu. Starters begin with avocado pear and white crabmeat with a ginger and cucumber mayonnaise, smoked salmon mousse with toasted granary bread, and a trio of deep-fried cheeses with a pink grapefruit conserve. There is a choice of about seven dishes for main course and these include chicken breast (filled with Sage Derby cheese on a sage butter sauce), leg of lamb steak (marinated in rosé wine) and fillet of beef en croûte (fillet steak in a pastry case served with a fresh tarragon sauce). The accompanying wine list numbers about 80 labels. All the major credit cards are accepted.

GROOMSLAND HOUSE RESTAURANT

Pulborough Road, Parbrook,
Billingshurst, Sussex RH14 9EU

Tel. (0403) 782571

THE SIR ROGER TICHBOURNE

Alfold Bars, Loxwood. Tel: (0403) 752377

Hours: *Open for bar meals lunchtime and dinner. No meals Mon lunch/Wed evening.*

Average Prices: *A la Carte £6.50; Sun lunch £3.25; snacks £1.*

Wines: *House wine £4.50 per bottle.*

Running south of the A281 from Horsham to Guildford, the B2133 cuts through a series of small country villages. The Sir Roger Tichbourne at Alfold Bars recalls local 19th century scandal, when a penniless Australian pretender to the Tichbourne baronetcy was found guilty of perjury and sentenced to ten years' hard labour. The inn itself is 15th century, with a beer garden, car park and also camping facilities in an adjacent field. Real ales — King and Barnes Sussex, Festive and Old Ale — are served from the bar with a traditional pub menu to accompany. Home-cooked ham, ploughman's lunches, salads, toasted sandwiches, jacket potatoes, steaks, breaded fish and pizzas are all served and supplemented by daily specials. Favourites include the house speciality, steak and kidney pie made with Old Ale, home-made chicken or prawn curry with rice, chicken Kiev, casseroled pork chops, or the popular tiger prawns served with salad, bread and butter and a Thousand Island dip. Smoked salmon or fresh Cromer crab salads are also popular. On Sunday there is always a traditional roast.

The Sir Roger Tichbourne
Loxwood
Tel: (0403) 752377

THE KINGS HEAD

Slinfold, near Horsham.
Tel: (0403) 790339

Hours:	*Open for lunch and dinner. Closed Sun evening.*
	Bar meals.
Average Prices:	*A la Carte £10–£12; Sun lunch £5.95; snacks £2.50.*
Wines:	*House wine £*

Slinfold is a small village a few miles east of the centre of Horsham and close to the A29. The Kings Head itself can be found in the centre of the village, its large garden bordering open farmland. The interior of the pub was refurbished in late 1988 and there is now a separate restaurant and also a family room. The restaurant seats 35, serving a traditional menu, supplemented by blackboard specials. Soup of the day, home-made pâté and toast, and garlic mushrooms give a flavour of the starter list, with char-grills featured for the main course. Here there is a full range of steaks, plus dishes such as rack of lamb with an apricot glaze, chicken Kiev, Dover sole and baked salmon with rosemary and garlic. A selection of trolley desserts concludes, with espresso, cappuccino or a speciality liqueur coffee to round off. Real ales, open fires and snacks such as lasagne and seafood salads are highlights of the bar. Accommodation is provided in four rooms. Access and Visa cards are both accepted.

The Kings Head
Telephone (0403) 790339

THE CHEQUERS INN

Rowhook, near Horsham.
Tel: (0403) 790480

Hours:	*Open for lunch and dinner daily.*
Average Prices:	*A la Carte £10; Sun lunch £5.50; snacks £3.55.*
Wines:	*House wine £5.25 per bottle.*

Rowhook is a tiny hamlet close to the Surrey border and on the edges of the once-great Wealden Forest of Anderida. The old Roman road, Stane Street, also runs to the east of the village. The Chequers itself has a lineage extending back to the 15th century, with many original beams intact and a huge open fireplace still warding off winter chills. There are two bars and a separate supper bar, housed in a recently-converted adjacent building. The regular menu is supplemented by blackboard daily specials and begins with appetisers such as garlic shrimps and crispy bacon, served with salad, and granary bread and deep-fried mushrooms. Main course dishes include chicken and onion tagliatelle, baked trout with almonds and honey-glazed gammon steak with peaches. There is a range of traditional home-made puddings and rich desserts like hot chocolate fudge cake with cream, as well as sorbets and cheese and biscuits. Even more seating is available outside on the terrace and in the gardens which have a children's play area. Access and Visa cards are both accepted.

The Chequers Inn

Telephone: Slinfold (0403) 790480

YE OLDE KINGS HEAD HOTEL

Carfax, Horsham.
Tel: (0403) 53126

Hours: *Open for coffee, lunch, tea and dinner (last orders 9.45pm).*

Average Prices: *A la Carte £13.75; Table d'Hôte £10.50; Sun lunch £7.95.*

Wines: *House wine £5.75 per bottle.*

Ye Olde Kings Head was built during the 16th century and today the character of its age is revealed in the deliberately olde worlde décor. A timbered minstrel's gallery provides a focal point to the hotel, surrounded by dark oak panelling, brass artefacts and comfortable chairs in which to sit back and soak up the atmosphere. The main restaurant is also of oak, with button-back chairs and a contrasting red colour scheme. The main à la carte selection is divided into fish, steak, meat and vegetable dishes, and examples of the thoughtful cuisine include pork in a Dijon mustard sauce, tournedos Kings Head-style (wrapped in bacon, fried in garlic and served with a croûton in a port wine, redcurrant jelly and game sauce), scampi and prawn risotto topped with Parmesan cheese, and vegetable and walnut pie. A coffee shop is open until 4.30pm daily for snacks, pastries, tea and coffee, and at lunchtime there is a buttery for snacks like lasagne, breaded scampi, chilli con carne and open sandwiches.

Carfax, Horsham, West Sussex RH12 1EG   Telephone: Horsham (0403) 53126

THE COUNTRYMAN INN

Whitehall, Shipley, near Horsham. Tel: (040 387) 383

Hours:	*Open for coffee, lunch and dinner (last orders 10.15pm). Bar meals.*
Average Prices:	*A la Carte £8.50; Table d'Hôte £11.50; snacks £1.95.*
Wines:	*House wine £4.95 per bottle.*

The River Adur cuts across the South Downs and beyond it, to the north, lies an area of rich pasture and woodland. Shipley, which means 'the place of the sheep pasture', is situated on the river's banks. The ruins of a castle, the largest lake in the South (Knepp Mill Pond) and a smock windmill all add to the village's considerable charm. The mill was once owned by the poet Hilaire Belloc who expressed his love for the area in the poem *The South Country*.

The Countryman Inn reflects this setting with its distinctive beamed interior, gleaming with horsebrasses, warmed by an inglenook fireplace and engrained with a very homely atmosphere. The inn is run by members of the Vaughan family and dates, in the main part, from the 18th century, with various extensions added over the years.

Today the restaurant adjoins the lounge bar and has a daily-changed menu chalked up on blackboards. Home-made soups make an appetising beginning, to be followed by a choice of fresh fish, prime steaks and special deep-dish Countryman pies with fillings such as lamb and rosemary, venison and steak and kidney. The accompanying wine list has over 40 labels to choose from, and amongst the desserts are apple strudel and syllabub. Vegetarians can enjoy lentil soup, vegetable bake or other thoughtful dishes. Children, meanwhile, can have smaller portions.

In the bar, staple menu items include lasagne verdi, fish pie, jumbo sausages and baked potatoes. These can be washed down with a pint of real ale; the bar offers a choice of Whitbread ales and Marston's Pedigree.

THE COUNTRYMAN INN

SHIPLEY
NR. HORSHAM
W. SUSSEX
RH13 8PZ

(just off A272)

TEL. COOLHAM 383
(040 387)

THE OLD FORGE RESTAURANT

6a Church Street, Storrington. Tel: (0903) 743402

Hours: *Open for lunch and dinner (last orders 9pm). Closed Sun evening/Mon.*

Average Prices: *A la Carte £16–£22; Table d'Hôte lunch £11; Sun lunch £11.*

Wines: *House wine £6 per bottle.*

Since Clive and Cathy Roberts took over The Old Forge, its reputation has been transformed into a cosy 22-seater restaurant which is memorable not only for its menu, but for the small touches which give any meal its roundness.

Pre-dinner drinks are served at the bar and are accompanied by canapés such as mini-quiches and cheese pasties, all home-made. The restaurant itself has a country freshness with exposed brickwork, fresh flowers and neat table linen. The setting serves to underscore a modern British menu which places great emphasis on freshness and thus changes monthly.

There is usually a choice of about four starters with, for example, tartlette of oak-smoked salmon, bound in lightly whipped Mascarpone cream cheese, and steamed rabbit and hazelnut pudding.

The main course features fish, game, beef and always one vegetarian dish. Typical of the choice is cannon of new season Southdown lamb,on a soubric of spinach with a light Madeira sauce, fillets of fresh Cornish skate with a Chardonnay sauce, flavoured with lemon and capers,or a warm gougère, flavoured with Gruyère cheese and filled with a ragoût of mushrooms, peppers and shallots.

To finish, there is a selection of British cheeses or appetising desserts, whilst to accompany the menu there is a small wine list.

The Old Forge

LICENSED RESTAURANT

6a Church Street
Storrington
West Sussex RH20 4LA
Telephone: (0903) 743402

THE COTTAGE TANDOORI

25 West Street, Storrington.
Tel: (090 66) 3605

Hours:	*Open for lunch and dinner (last orders 11.30pm).*
Average Prices:	*A la Carte £10.*
Wines:	*House wine £5.50 per bottle.*

The Cottage Tandoori is a skilful blend of highly English setting with quality Indian cuisine. The restaurant is a Georgian conversion, furnished in deep red and with many interesting alcoves. The menu is comprehensive and particularly helpful for the inexperienced, as it gives a careful explanation of the various Indian cooking styles. The whole range of curries are covered: dupiaza (medium, with onions and a distinctive taste), bhuna (spicy, with fresh tomatoes and dhania leaves) and dhansak (mild, with lentils, lemon and aromatic herbs). Specialities of the house include tandoori dishes, jafrey dishes (chicken, meat or king prawns barbecued tandoori-style and then cooked in a spicy sauce with pure butter) and korai dishes (lamb, chicken or king prawns cooked in a thick blend of sauces and flared in the korai). Khurzi chicken or lamb can be prepared for parties of three to four but requires 24 hours' notice. Service is courteous and attentive, and booking is advised for the weekends. An enlarged cocktail bar is a new addition.

Telephone Storrington 3605 & 5974

THE FRANKLAND ARMS

Old London Road, Washington. Tel: (0903) 892220

Hours: *Open for dinner, Wed–Sat, and Sun lunch.*
Bar meals lunchtime and evening every day.

Average Prices: A la Carte £9.50 (bar), £12.50 (restaurant)

The Frankland Arms is a popular pub with walkers along the South Downs Way. Many come down to the village having climbed up to the Iron Age hillfort, Chanctonbury Ring, which has sweeping views out over the Downs. The inn has a gas-lit à la carte restaurant and also serves a popular selection of bar snacks. Home-made pies, steaks, fish and poultry are always available, as well as a choice of some of Whitbread's real ales.

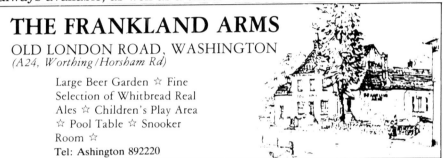

THE FRANKLAND ARMS
OLD LONDON ROAD, WASHINGTON
(A24, Worthing/Horsham Rd)

Large Beer Garden ☆ Fine
Selection of Whitbread Real
Ales ☆ Children's Play Area
☆ Pool Table ☆ Snooker
Room ☆
Tel: Ashington 892220

THE BRIDGE INN

Houghton Bridge, Amberley. Tel: (0798) 831619

Hours: *Open for lunch and dinner.*

Average Prices: A la Carte £6.

The Bridge Inn is situated on the South Downs Way, close to the River Arun and right in the heart of the Sussex countryside. The inn provides bed and breakfast accommodation for the walkers on the long distance bridle path, has summer barbecues and is a free house with a fine selection of real ales. Home-made pies feature on the snack menu which offers half-prices for children. Parties are also catered for.

THE BRIDGE INN
HOUGHTON BRIDGE, AMBERLEY

Beer Garden ☆ Summer Bar-B-Cues
☆ Riverside Walks ☆ Bed & Breakfast
Close to Chalk Pits Museum, Arundel, Fontwell
and Goodwood

Tel: Bury 831619

THE OLD SMITHY

Old London Road, Washington. Tel: (0903) 892271

Hours: *Open for coffee, lunch and dinner. Closed Sun evening/Mon.*

Average Prices: *A la Carte £20; Table d'Hôte lunch £9.25, dinner £14.95; Sun lunch £9.95.*

Wines: *House wine from £6.35 per bottle.*

The Old Smithy can be found just out of Washington on the A24, which runs up through the Downs from Worthing to Horsham. The Old Smithy is a popular stopping-off point with both passing motorists and visitors to the ancient monuments of the area. To cope with a steadily increasing demand, an airy conservatory has been added, leading off the main oak-beamed restaurant. The aim of proprietors Barry and Carol Froggatt is to provide reasonably-priced food in large helpings. Starters include a smoked salmon platter garnished with lemon and king prawns, melon with raspberries, and pâté-stuffed mushrooms. A number of steak dishes feature on the main course, along with pork fillet Madeira, Dover sole Colbert (topped with prawns and asparagus) and braised wood pigeon (cooked in a Burgundy sauce with deep-fried croûtons). Sunday lunch sees traditional roast beef with Yorkshire pudding, roast turkey with seasoning and a chipolata sausage, or local trout with almonds. A sweet trolley and coffee and mints conclude.

The
Old Smithy

Tel:
Washington
(0903) 892271

ᏟᎻᎬ SᎷᏌᏳᏳᏞᎬᎡᏚ

West Street, Sompting.
Tel: Worthing (0903) 36072

Hours: Open for coffee, lunch and dinner. Closed Sun evening/Mon.

Average Prices: A la Carte £13.50; Table d'Hôte lunch £7.95; Sun lunch £8.95.

A 10th century Saxon church tower and a long tradition of smuggling make Sompting a village with a colourful past. The aptly named Smugglers Restaurant maintains this link with the sea, as a speciality fish restaurant serving scallops, lobster, John Dory and calamari to name but a few dishes. It also provides a wide range of coffees, including Jamaican (rum coffee).

Mill House Hotel

Mill Lane, Ashington.
Tel: Ashington (0903) 892426

Hours: Open for coffee, lunch, tea and dinner.

Average Prices: A la Carte £13.50; Sun lunch £8.95.

Midway between Horsham and Worthing, this country hotel enjoys a quiet setting just off the main road (A24). It offers a comprehensive menu for both starters and main courses, with Sunday lunches a speciality. Lemon and turmeric chicken, pork in apple and cider, and veal with a hazelnut sauce are among the many dishes. There is also a pleasant garden for summer drinking and the hotel is widely recommended.

GEORGE'S CARVERY

Old London Road, Washington. Tel: (0903) 892947
Hours: *Open for coffee, lunch and dinner (last orders 10pm). Closed all day Mon and Sun/Tues evenings.*
Average Prices: *A la Carte £18; Table d'Hôte carvery £10–£12.50.*

George's Carvery has the pleasant atmosphere of a house in the country. In addition to the carvery, there is a separate à la carte selection, with, amongst the dishes, breast of duck with a blackcurrant and red wine coulis, and grilled scallops wrapped in bacon, served on a bed of tagliatelle with a Cointreau sauce.

George's Carvery

LICENSED RESTAURANT

LONDON ROAD,

WASHINGTON,

W. SUSSEX

TEL: WASHINGTON 892947

THE FOUNTAIN INN

Ashurst, Steyning. Tel: (0403) 710219
Hours: *Open for bar meals lunchtime and evening. No meals Wed/Sun evenings.*
Average Prices: *Snacks from £2.25; house wine £5.45 per bottle.*

Lattice windows, hanging plants and a whitewashed exterior welcome guests to The Fountain Inn. It dates back over 400 years and has an inglenook fireplace. The range of pub fare displayed on the blackboard includes salmon or chicken en croûte, moussaka, steaks and smoked ham. Vegetarians are catered for. Five real ales are served.

Fountain Inn

ASHURST
STEYNING
SUSSEX
Telephone
Partridge Green
710219

The Parsonage
IN TARRING VILLAGE

6–10 High Street, Tarring, Worthing, West Sussex,
BN14 7NN

Telephone 0903 820140   VAT No. 459 6097 02

THE CASTLE HOTEL

The Street, Bramber. Tel: (0903) 812102

Hours: *Open for lunch and dinner (last orders 9.30pm).*
Closed Sun evening.

Average Prices: *A la Carte £10; Sun lunch £6; snacks from 90p.*

The Castle Hotel makes a convenient base for rambling on the
surrounding Downlands, whilst the village of Bramber itself is interesting
for its unusual pipe museum. The hotel has a 17th century restaurant
which serves a full selection of Anglo-French dishes, supplemented by
blackboard specials. Gourmets, vegetarians, children and the just plain
hungry all find a welcome. Ample car parking.

THE OLD TOLLGATE RESTAURANT

The Street, Bramber, Steyning.
Tel: (0903) 813362/815104

Hours: *Open for lunch, 12–2pm, and dinner, 7–10pm. Closed Sun evening.*

Average Prices: *Lunch £8.75/£10.55 (2/3 courses); dinner £12.55.*

Wines: *House wine from £6.50 per litre; 90p per glass.*

The great popularity of The Old Tollgate Restaurant stems from its truly original English menu, served against an authentically recreated Edwardian backdrop. The atmosphere of an old mill, with its wooden floors, oak doors, lantern lights and solid wooden tables and chairs, never fails to draw in the many visitors to the area and makes booking advisable. Even the menu style is reminiscent of theatre posters of the era offering "lamb, beef and pork, chicken, guinea fowl and hare and other creatures of farm and field, fishy delights and other satisfying dishes". The choice is indeed comprehensive offering roasts from the carvery, casseroles, savoury pies and vegetarian dishes, followed by fresh fruit puddings, pies, creams, sauces and — as they put it — "other sweet delights". There is great insistence on everything being fresh at The Old Tollgate, for, as the menu says, "here is a place of welcome where plain but wholesome dishes of home-grown produce and dairy foods are cooked with diligence".

TOTTINGTON MANOR HOTEL AND RESTAURANT

Edburton, near Henfield. Tel: (0903) 815757

Hours: *Open for coffee, lunch and dinner (last orders 9.30pm). Bar meals daily; restaurant open Wed–Sat.*

Average Prices: A la Carte dinner £22. House wine £7 per bottle.

Tottington Manor is an ideal base from which to enjoy the character and countryside of the surrounding downlands, offering guests the oportunity to unwind in an atmosphere of relaxation.

Run by Kate and David Miller, there are six bedrooms (all en suite), a 45-seater restaurant, and a function room for up to 20. David is a noted chef whose career has spanned Gleneagles Hotel in Scotland and The Royal Garden, Sheraton Park and The Ritz in London, where he worked as head chef.

Quality is assured on à la carte selection, which might begin with appetisers such as Scotch salmon (marinated with fresh dill and accompanied by a crisp fennel and quail egg salad), or terrine of freshwater eels (bound with a vegetable mousse and served with a herb and tomato dressing).

Main courses cover fish, char-grills and meat. Fresh scallops (baked in a creamy sauce flavoured with tarragon and English mustard), roast best end of new season Southdown lamb (with Dijon mustard and herb breadcrumbs, garnished with savoury tomatoes and lamb gravy) and scampis in love (pan-fried scampi and tender fillet of veal flamed in Pernod and simmered in cream with shallots and parsley) are all typical of the choice. Desserts from the table may feature the dish of seasonal fruits and berries glazed with a mandarin Napoleon liqueur sauce, as well as a fine selection of gâteaux.

Cigar and pipe smoking is discouraged in the restaurant. An excellent choice of bar food and real ales is available seven days a week.

Tottington Manor Hotel & Restaurant

Edburton, Nr. Henfield, Sussex, BN5 9LJ. Telephone Steyning (0903) 815757

David & Kate Miller

ST PETERS COTTAGE RESTAURANT

Cowfold, near Horsham. Tel: (0403) 864324

Hours: *Open for coffee, lunch and dinner. Closed Sun evening/Mon.*

Average Prices: Table d'Hôte lunch £6.75; Sun lunch £7.25.

Between Haywards Heath and Billingshurst, the A272 runs through Cowfold. St Peters Cottage has stood here since the 13th century when it was believed to have been a priest's house. Today it serves a menu which ranges over fish, poultry, steak and vegetarian dishes. Try the popular salmon St Peters-style (served with a green pepper sauce), or plaice mandarin.

THE JAMES KING

Horsham Road, Pease Pottage. Tel: (0293) 27140/612261

Hours: *Open for lunch and dinner. Closed Sun/Mon.*

Average Prices: Set dinner £14.95; lunch £12.95; snacks from £2.50.

The James King is suitably geared to both family parties and businessmen. The informal Sussex Kitchen serves a wide range of meals and has a help-yourself salad bar. The separate 40-cover restaurant offers a menu which may begin with crown of melon with a trio of sorbets, and follow with fresh salmon or the James King Special (sandwich of beef, ham and turkey coated with mustard and infilled with Mozzarella).

ALEXANDER HOUSE

Turners Hill, West Sussex
Telephone Copthorne (0342) 714914 & 716333

ALEXANDER HOUSE HOTEL

Turners Hill, near Copthorne.
Tel: (0342) 714914

Hours:	*Open for morning coffee, lunch, afternoon tea and dinner (last orders 9.30pm, 9pm Sun). No bar meals Sun.*
Average Prices:	*A la Carte £30; Table d'Hôte £35; bar snacks from £2.*
Wines:	*House wine £11.50 per bottle.*

Alexander House enshrines all that once made Sussex one of the wealthiest and most cultured regions of England. The legacy of royalty, nobility and statesmen to the county has been a scattering of impressive mansion houses, set against a backdrop of immaculately tended gardens and rolling downland. Alexander House is one of the few private mansions remaining and every effort has been made by its present owners to ensure that visitors are treated as personal houseguests. Butler service, afternoon tea over a game of croquet, the buzz of an early evening cocktail party and a quiet game of backgammon in the library, all suggest an aura of Edwardian country high-living. The public rooms each possess a mellow décor, combining a restrained opulence with comfortable elegance.

The dining room, for example, has the refinement of the Georgian era, with its oval-backed padded chairs, ruched curtains, wall panelling and silver service. Where the cuisine is concerned, chef Francis Baumer and his team have carefully crafted an imaginative and polished menu. Typical starters might include rillette de canard aux champignons sauvages (coarse duck pâté with a tartlet of hot wild mushrooms), or salade exotique de coquilles et de homard (scallop and lobster salad with melon, avocado and caviar butter).

The main course is divided into les poissons and les viandes. Dishes include saumon et raviolis aux langoustines, sauce orange (pan-fried salmon with langoustine ravioli and orange sauce), filet de boeuf à la mousse de Stilton et de poireaux (fillet of beef with a Stilton, leek and peppercorn mousse and a rich red wine sauce) and filet de veau aux nouilles et jambon de Parme, sauce tomate (fillet of veal on home-made noodles with Parma ham and a tomato and yoghurt coulis). The dessert list is both varied and delicate in composition. Try, perhaps, mousse de poires amandine, sauce chocolat (pear mousse on an almond and chocolate base with a chocolate sauce), or pêches fourrées au soufflé de la passiflore (peaches with a light passion fruit soufflé).

Each meal becomes an experience in itself and can be rounded off with cigars and vintage liqueurs served in the library. In keeping with house tradition, jacket and tie are required for dinner. Chauffeured limousines and a helipad are also on hand, particularly useful for guests wishing to travel to nearby Gatwick Airport. Conferences and weddings are also catered for.

THE RED LION

High Street, Lindfield.
Tel: (044 47) 3152

Hours: *Open for bar meals 11am–9.30pm, Mon–Sat. Lunch 12–2pm and dinner 7–9.30pm.*

Average Prices: *A la Carte £7–£10; Sun lunch £4.50; snacks from £1.40.*

Wines: *From £6 per bottle.*

Family-run by the Simpsons, the stated aim of The Red Lion at Lindfield is to cater for those who appreciate the good old-fashioned values which have made the hostelries of Britain the envy of the world. A 1,000-year-old yew tree stands in the garden of this inn, which was built in 1637 and was once the haunt of smugglers. Some years ago, when alterations were being made, a wall was knocked down to reveal a secret hoard of casks of brandy and port. Today the food is all home-made, fresh and English in style. Steaks, lamb cutlets, mixed grills, roast chicken and poached salmon are some of the main course examples. Starters of home-made soup, pâté with toast and whitebait also lead on to seafood dishes which include fresh cod and plaice. There's a fine range of cold platters, with all the trimmings, and daily chef's specials. The speciality of the house is The Red Lion mixed grill, — it has everything. The garden is also a pleasure and the outdoor covered barbecue is reckoned to be one of the best in Sussex. Visa and Access cards are welcomed, as are Luncheon Vouchers.

The Complete Pub for all the family — Warm Friendly Atmosphere

Try our chef's special home-made dishes. *Bar meals available.* *11.00am–9.30pm Mon–Sat* *Luncheon 12.00–2.00pm* *Dinner 7.00–9.30pm* *Visa, Access, LV's Accepted*	*ACCOMMODATION* *Luxurious Rooms with Colour TV* *Tea & Coffee making facilities* *En suite Bathrooms* *Single: £35 per night. Double: £45 per night* *Includes Continental Breakfast* *Full English Breakfast available at extra cost.*	*Darts, Bar Billiards, Pool, Dominoes and Crib.* *Large Gardens.* *Draught Bass & IPA.* *Pub open 10.30am–11.00pm* *Mon–Sat; 12.00–3.00pm and* *7.00–10.30pm Sundays.*

HIGH STREET, LINDFIELD. TEL: LINDFIELD 3152

effingham park

The Wellingtonia à la carte restaurant

The Wellingtonia offers an extensive selection from the Carte du Jour, and is ideal for the Business Executive if time is of the essence.

The Wellingtonia is not the only facility available at Effingham Park; after your meal it is possible to enjoy a relaxing walk through the gardens, or for the more energetic we have our own 9 hole Golf Course (nominal green fees apply), Putting Green, Croquet Lawn and extensive Leisure Club with swimming pool, saunas, jacuzzi and Turkish Baths — day membership is available to visitors.

EFFINGHAM PARK, WEST PARK ROAD, COPTHORNE, WEST SUSSEX.
Restaurant: (0342) 717559   Hotel: (0342) 714994

EFFINGHAM PARK

West Park Road, Copthorne.
Tel: (0342) 717599/714994

Hours:	*Open for lunch and dinner. Restaurant closed Sat lunch/all day Sun.*
Average Prices:	*A la Carte £20; Carte du Jour £15.00.(lunch only)*
Wines:	*House wine £9.25 per bottle.*

Effingham Park, which opened in September 1988, is a hotel which aims to make business and leisure a pleasure, and preferably the two in tandem. 40 acres of parkland, a wealth of amenities (including a leisure club, a croquet lawn and a nine hole golf course) and a design on a grand scale contribute toa striking first impression. The Wellingtonia has its own separate entrance and is named after the Wellingtonia trees which line its driveway. The décor is relaxing and modern; elegance is the keynote. Large, delicately arched windows, which overlook the gardens, and pale pink napery create a relaxing backdrop to the culinary skills of the team of chefs who present a selection of dishes à la carte, as well as a carte du jour. The hotel is located on B2028, half a mile off the main A264 and close to junction 10 of the M23.

VINYARDS WINE BAR

42 High Street, Hurstpierpoint. Tel: (0273) 835000

Hours: *Open for coffee, lunch and dinner (last orders*
                10pm). Bar meals.
Average Prices: *A la Carte £9.95; Sun lunch £4.95; snacks from £1.50.*
Wines: *House wine £5.50 per bottle.*

Long relaxing meals eaten al fresco as the sun slowly sets are not
traditionally the preserve of Britain's bistros and wine bars. At Vinyards,
however, new proprietors Mark and Jane Cooper have made determined
efforts to lend their premises a Continental atmosphere. Vinyards is open
all day on Friday (and pub hours the rest of the week) for coffee, tea, light
snacks and full meals, and the courtyard to the rear, looking south over the
Downs with sun all day and evening, is an ideal setting for informal
gatherings, or in which to enjoy a quiet drink over the day's newspapers.
The menu is seasonally adjusted but concentrates on bistro-style fare.
Jacket potatoes, for example, come with about 16 different fillings,
including cheese and chilli, mustard butter, and baked beans with crispy
bacon. The selection of salads features prawns, crab and salmon, and
other popular dishes include spicy chilli on rice, tuna bake, Japanese
prawns with salad, seafood lasagne and, for vegetarians, mushroom nut
fettuccine with salad. Desserts are deliberately rich, offering a Caribbean
calypso gâteau, banoffi pie and raspberry trifle. Vinyards is always at its
busiest between 5.30 and 6.30pm, the 'adjustment' hour, when £1 is
knocked off a bottle of wine and doubles are charged at the single price.
On Monday–Thursday lunchtimes parties of four and over receive a
half-litre carafe of house wine. The wine bar can also cater for private
functions. Once a month there is usually a theme night (such as Hawaiian
or Cockney) and, during summer, barbecues are held every Saturday
evening and Sunday lunchtime.

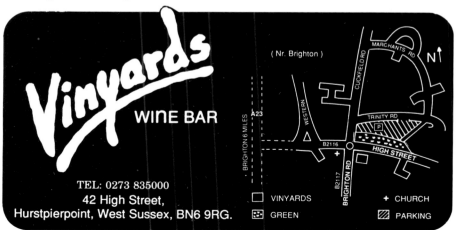

67

THE WHITE HORSE INN

High Street, Hurstpierpoint.
Tel: (0273) 834717
Hours: *Open all day.*
Average Prices: *A la Carte from £8.50; Sun lunch £6.95.*
Wines: *House wine £5.25 per bottle.*

A warm and friendly welcome is what visitors find at The White Horse Inn, a pub and restaurant which recently came third in a 'Pub of the Year 1989' competition. This 16th century coaching inn, complete with an original oak-beamed restaurant, serves a good selection of dishes à la carte, prepared from produce from local suppliers. These range from T-bone steaks to Dover sole, with specials which change daily. Duck à l'orange, venison in red wine, pork Pompeii, home-made steak and kidney pudding mountain, chicken stuffed with crab and pink peppercorns, and veal cordon bleu have all featured. For the less adventurous there is a full range of bar meals which can be enjoyed either in the comfortable lounge bar, with its picture gallery and homely atmosphere, or in the Garden Bar where pool or darts can be played. Real ales, strong lager and fine wines and spirits are served in a convivial atmosphere, and all the leading credit cards are taken. The White Horse can be found on the edge of Hurstpierpoint, coming from the A23. There is a beer garden and ample car parking.

The White Horse Inn, Hurstpierpoint, West Sussex. Tel: (0273) 834717

THE GRAND

King's Road, Brighton.
Tel: (0273) 21188   Fax: (0273) 202694

Hours: *Open for meals all day (last orders 10pm).*
Average Prices: *A la Carte £19.50–£30; Table d'Hôte lunch £14.50, dinner*
                    £19.50.
Wines: *From £9.50 per bottle.*

It has been said that The Grand typifies all that is good in an English luxury
hotel, and its dining opportunities are many. The well known King's
Restaurant presents a dinner menu which is rich in imagination. Begin
with a chicken liver parfait, served on French leaves with a warm walnut
vinaigrette, or perhaps a terrine of crab and salmon mousse with a Marie
Rose sauce. Main courses offer Scottish beef with a perigourdine sauce,
julienne of rabbit in an oyster mushroom sauce, served on spinach in a
puff pastry parcel, and fillet of pork with a grain mustard sauce and pine
kernels. Even more exotic is the chef's Celebration Menu, displaying
choices like tournedos de boeuf pot-au-feu avec foie gras et sauce Madère
(pot roasted tournedos of beef with foie gras and Madeira sauce). Less
extravagant is The Victoria Lounge menu, which ranges from sandwiches
and salads to goujons of lemon sole, and afternoon tea is a special
occasion, to be enjoyed at £7.50. A regular dinner dance is held every
Saturday night and there's a traditional lunch on Sundays. All is to be
enjoyed in a setting of quiet elegance and sophistication.

—— THE GRAND BRIGHTON ——

THE GRAND, KING'S ROAD, BRIGHTON, EAST SUSSEX.

DEANS PLACE HOTEL

Alfriston, Polegate.
Tel: (0323) 870248/870450 (guests)   Fax: (0323) 870918

Hours: *Open for coffee, lunch, tea and dinner (last orders 9pm).*

Average Prices: *A la Carte £12–£15; Table d'Hôte £11.75; bar meals from £1.25.*

Wines: *From £6 per bottle.*

Deans Place Hotel, set in the charming village of Alfriston in the Cuckmere Valley, is a beautifully appointed, three star country house hotel. 40 en suite bedrooms, with full modern facilities, are accompanied by excellent sporting amenities and fine gardens. Conference and function facilities are available for up 150 guests (200 buffet style), whilst The Gallery Restaurant seats 110 diners in spacious comfort. The à la carte selection spans most tastes and includes ten house specialities, whilst the daily table d'hôte menu features five or six starters and main courses such as supreme of chicken, roast rack of Southdown lamb, sirloin steak garni and poached darne of salmon with a creamy seafood sauce. There is a fine choice of bar meals too, from a simple sandwich or ploughman's lunch to salads and hot meals like steak and kidney pie and locally-caught fillet of plaice. All leading credit cards are taken, with the exception of Diner's Club. The special 'Sussex Weekend Breaks' are worth enquiring about.

ALFRISTON
POLEGATE
TEL: (0323) 870248 (Office)
(0323) 870450 (Guests)

DEANS
PLACE
HOTEL
★ ★ ★

THE STAR INN

High Street, Alfriston.
Tel: (0323) 870495   Fax: (0323) 870922

Hours: *Open for coffee, lunch, tea and dinner (last orders 9.30pm).*

Average Prices: *A la Carte £15; Table d'Hôte £11.*

Wines: *From £6.95 per bottle.*

This historic Trusthouse Forte establishment is famous throughout the country and, set as it is, in one of the loveliest villages in England, it is small wonder that it has become so very popular. There is more to The Star, however, than its picture-book image; the restaurant is another attraction, offering traditional English fare which ranges from fresh brook trout and rosettes of Southdown lamb to Dover sole and Scottish salmon. The steaks and lamb cutlets are house specialities and the breast of chicken and escalope of veal are original. The Star's 'Smuggler's Pie' is from a secret recipe which has been handed down for over a century, whilst amongst the starters there is a country herb pâté, made with fresh cream and sherry, prawn and crab cascade and South Coast mussels, grilled with a savoury topping of shallots and garlic butter. The fixed price lunch menus are considered great value, with a choice of five starters and half-a-dozen main courses each day. All leading credit cards are accepted.

High Street, Alfriston. Tel: (0323) 870495

TALLY HO!

42 Church Street, Eastbourne.
Tel: (0323) 32083

Hours: *Open for coffee, lunch and dinner (last orders 10.15pm).*

Average Prices: *A la Carte £12.55; set lunch £6.25; bar meals from £2.25.*

Wines: *From £5 per bottle; £1 per glass.*

One of the most interesting and attractive pubs in the county, with its colourful hunting-scene frieze over the front entrance, the Tally Ho! has a fine reputation for its home-cooking and real ales. Sheila and Michael Pooley, together with son Neil (an accomplished chef who supervises the kitchen operations), deliberately set out to create a first class pub serving good food, rather than an inn disguised as a restaurant. The restaurant itself seats 35 in spacious and elegant surroundings, and meals are available in the bar too. The use of local suppliers of vegetables, fruit, meat and fish ensures daily freshness, a priority of the inn. The steaks are particularly popular, ranging from fillet to sirloin and rump, and there are home-made steak and kidney pie, fresh plaice, trout, cod and seafood platters, whilst the bar menu of lighter meals offers scampi in the basket, omelettes, ham and eggs, and freshly cut sandwiches. Reasonable prices and a friendly atmosphere complete the scene. Visa cards are welcome.

TALLY HO!

42 Church Street, Eastbourne
Tel: (0323) 32083

THE GRAND HOTEL

King Edward's Parade, Eastbourne.
Tel: (0323) 412345   Fax: (0323) 412233

Hours: *Open for lunch, tea and dinner. Mirabelle closed Sun.*
Average Prices: *Mirabelle: A la Carte £30; Table d'Hôte lunch £15, dinner £24.50.*
Wines: *From £9 per bottle.*

Introducing guests to The Grand, the hotel's brochure says "Five star? Most people put The Grand above that sort of classification. It is too atmospheric, too legendary, too individual to be bracketed." This indeed sums up the esteem in which it is held. To diners the lovely Garden Restaurant is already well known. Now there is a brand new restaurant, The Mirabelle. Elegant and sophisticated, it is already much talked about. Guests can choose à la carte from a menu which changes with the seasons but offers some seven starters and a similar number of main courses, including perhaps venison, Gressingham duck, veal sweetbreads, rack of English lamb and prime Scottish beef. Alternatively, the table d'hôte is tempting, with dishes like light soup of mussels with saffron and capsicums, followed by paupiettes of pork wrapped in smoked bacon and braised with young sage leaves, garnished with sautéed apples, or supreme of Scottish salmon with a compote of tomatoes and herbs. The wine list is expertly compiled.

The Grand Hotel. King Edward's Parade Eastbourne Sussex BN21 4EQ
Telephone (0323) 412345 Telex 87332 Telefax 412233

73

THE HOLE IN THE WALL

Pelham Yard, High Street, Seaford. Tel: (0323) 893785

Hours: *Open 10.30am–11pm (last orders 10pm).*

Average Prices: *A la Carte £7.50–£12; Table d'Hôte £7.50; bar meals from £1.50.*

Wines: *From £4.50 per bottle.*

This lovely 18th century inn is one of Seaford's main attractions. After two gold awards in Charrington's good food scheme and a pub caterer of the year award in 1986, the inn has just picked up another accolade for owners John and June Boots, that of Regional Wine Restaurateur. John and June are third generation publicans and it is their experience, coupled with the expertise of their team, which has made The Hole in the Wall one of the most popular inns in the South. The fare is traditional English in style, but with some Continental influences, and the bar meals include moussaka, chicken hot pot, fillet of plaice or cod, seafood platters and a whole range of fine salads, as well as favourites like ham and eggs, steak sandwiches and home-made steak and kidney pie with mushrooms. The à la carte selection offers Aberdeen Angus steaks — cut to various sizes up to 24oz if required! — prime T-bones and steak au poivre, alongside fresh fish, mixed grills and more. Gâteaux, trifles and sundaes are all home-made. The table d'hôte lunch has two courses for £7.50. Visa and Access cards are welcome.

CHARRINGTON
GOOD FOOD HOUSE

Hole in the Wall

CIRCA 1790
PELHAM YARD
HIGH ST.
SEAFORD
(0323) 893785

PUB CATERER
1986
HIGHLY COMMENDED

THE DORSET ARMS

22 Malling Street, Lewes.
Tel: (0273) 477110

Hours: *Open for coffee, lunch and dinner (last orders 10pm).*
     Open all day in summer.

Average Prices: A la Carte £9.50; Sun lunch £4.50; bar meals from £1.15.

Wines: *£2.90 per half-litre; £5.60 per litre.*

With a reputation for food to equal that of almost any restaurant or inn in this part of the county, The Dorset Arms offers fine variety on its menus. Steaks are specialities and are in great demand, cut from well-hung whole sides. Diners can have an 8oz or a 12oz, or even just a steak sandwich. Fish is almost as popular, especially on Friday, fish day, when the catch is brought direct from Newhaven. Other temptations include steak and kidney pie, game pie, a choice of salads and light bites like ploughman's lunches and sandwiches. For dessert there is the banana, toffee and biscuit concoction, banoffi pie, and a hot butterscotch and walnut pudding. Over 60 wines accompany the menu and the traditional Sussex ales are Armada Ale, Best Bitter, IPA and Mild, all from Harvey's brewery, itself based in Lewes. Double rooms with showers and colour TVs are available for those looking to stay longer. Access, Visa and American Express cards are welcomed.

THE DORSET ARMS
22 MALLING ST, LEWES (0273) 477110

Shelleys Hotel

and THE VINE RESTAURANT

at

Lewes, East Sussex

tel. (0273) 472361/2

SHELLEY'S HOTEL AND THE VINE RESTAURANT

Lewes.
Tel: (0273) 472361/2

Hours: *Open for coffee, lunch, tea and dinner (last orders 9pm).*

Average Prices: *A la Carte £14; Table d'Hôte £13.50; Sun lunch £11.50; bar meals from £1.50.*

Wines: *From £7.85 per bottle.*

The history of Shelley's goes back to medieval times when it was a part of the borough of the manor of Lewes. The Vyne Inn was built on this freehold in 1526, with the Renaissance porch built by the then innkeeper (one Thomas Pellard), still surviving to this day. The property was later acquired by the Earls of Dorset and then by other notables until it was sold in 1633 to the Shelley family.

During the first world war the house was used as a military hospital for officers and became a hotel in 1932. It was purchased by the progressive Mount Charlotte group in 1977, since when, following extensive refurbishment, it has become known as one of the most attractive country house hotels in the county.

One of the features of Shelley's is the superb collection of fine antique furnishings which grace the hotel and the paintings and prints which adorn the walls. In addition, there are 21 bedrooms, all with bathrooms or showers en suite, and a 24 hour room service is provided. In short, there is every facility for functions from weddings to business seminars and gourmet weekends.

The Vine Restaurant has a first class reputation and the following examples, taken from a menu which changes regularly, give some idea of the style of the cuisine. Starters include crispy squid with a tomato and garlic sauce, French onion soup, country garden mushrooms in a horseradish and cream sauce, and spiced avocado pear. Main course offers some 14 choices, with lobster thermidor, baked trout, lemon sole, halibut, breast of duck in a kumquat sauce and chateaubriand being amongst the favourites. A selection of sweets and a cheeseboard conclude and there is a very respectable wine list featuring 45 vintages and non-vintages. A traditional lunch is available on Sundays.

Meals are only served in the bar at lunchtimes. The hotel's breakfasts are well known: freshly squeezed orange juice, fresh grapefruit and a choice of cereals, to be followed by kippers or the great British breakfast, comprising bacon, farm eggs, kidneys, sausages, tomatoes and mushrooms, and accompanied by Indian or China tea, coffee, hot chocolate or even Bovril.

All major credit cards are welcomed.

THE PELHAM ARMS

High Street, Lewes. Tel: (0273) 476149

Hours: *Open for lunch and dinner (last orders 9.45pm).*
Closed Mon lunchtime.

Average Prices: A la Carte £9.50; Sun lunch £6.95.

Situated at the top of the High Street, The Pelham Arms dates from around 1640 and is, today, a popular local, particularly at lunchtime when its Sussex Kitchen Restaurant is always busy with regulars, tourists and businessmen. Typical of the menu choice are Pelham pie, mixed seafood casserole and the Pelham pot au chocolat. The bar is large but cosy and the list of bar meals changes daily. Real ales on draught.

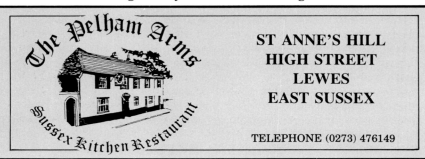

ST ANNE'S HILL
HIGH STREET
LEWES
EAST SUSSEX

TELEPHONE (0273) 476149

THE OLD POLEGATE STATION

Station Road, Polegate.
Tel: (032 12) 2172

Hours: *Open 8am–11pm for breakfast, coffee, lunch, tea and dinner (last orders 10pm).*

Average Prices: £1–£8.

Wines: *House wine £3.20 per half-litre; £6.40 per litre.*

Modern, efficient and attractive, The Old Polegate Station is one of Whitbread's Brewers Fayre houses. Once an important railway station, this is now a beautifully modernised inn, offering food throughout the day. The standard menu, as with all Brewers Fayre houses, offers plenty of choice. Appetisers include favourites like prawn cocktail, home-made soup, farmhouse pâté with hot toast and hot mushrooms, coated, deep-fried and served with a special dip. The main courses are called 'Hot Platters'. They are essentially a full meal, with steak and kidney pie, 8oz gammon steak, roast half-chicken, scampi, half-pound sirloin steak, fillet of plaice and Cumberland sausage (a giant, spicy sausage which has become a favourite). There is a complete range of fresh salad platters and 'Light Bites' (open or closed sandwiches) for those who want less than a full meal. A selection of desserts rounds off, there are sensibly priced wines and every day a specials menu is shown on the blackboard. Visa and Access cards are welcomed and there is plenty of parking.

THE OLD POLEGATE STATION

Station Road · Polegate · Tel: (032 12) 2172

THE STAR INN

Norman's Bay, Pevensey.
Tel: (0323) 762648

Hours: *Open for coffee, lunch and dinner (last orders 10pm).*
Average Prices: *£1.50–£7.50.*
Wines: *From £4 per bottle.*

This incredibly busy and successful inn, steeped in history and over 500 years old, is perhaps the most famous inn to be associated with smuggling in the entire country. It was here that the bloodiest of all battles between the smugglers and the revenue men took place, culminating in the last recorded 'run' which began on the night of January 3, 1828. This time the smugglers numbered an amazing 200. They landed their cargo in the bay but at Sidley Green they met with a blockade of 40 armed customs men and, whilst they got through, they left very many dead and it was effectively the end of an era which lasted right through from 1607. Still as full of character and atmosphere as ever, The Star Inn is as well known today for its food as for its history and has picked up many recommendations. The menu has sufficient variety to cater for all tastes, with starters like escargots, corn-on-the-cob, home-made soups, pâté and hot garlic mushrooms, to be followed by salads, steaks, seafoods, Stroganoffs and more. Comprehensive wine list and sensible prices.

Star Inn · Norman's Bay, Pevensey. Tel: (0323) 762648

COOPERS

Hailsham Road, Stone Cross, near Hailsham.
Tel: (0323) 763212

Hours: *Open 10.30am–11pm for coffee, lunch and dinner (last orders 10pm).*

Average Prices: *£1–£12.*

Wines: *From £3.20 per bottle.*

It is a pleasant surprise to discover a spacious and elegant restaurant/public house like this in such a country setting. Standing in its own grounds, with wide lawns, shady trees and a large car park, Coopers is one of the Brewers Fayre establishments. Opened in summer 1989, it has all modern facilities, including a special children's room and a fully equipped playground. To drink there are real ales, and the well-known Brewers Fayre menu offers favourites such as 'light bites' of open (or closed) sandwiches on brown or white bread (with roast beef, home-cooked ham, poached salmon, prawn or English cheese) and hot platters like steak and kidney pie, roast half-chicken, scampi, breaded plaice and steaks, as well as salads and daily specials which are declared on the blackboard. To accompany the meal, over a dozen wines have been selected, each helpfully starred on the list according to its lightness and sweetness. Meals are served every day of the week and Visa and Access cards are welcomed.

COOPERS

STONE CROSS   *HAILSHAM*

TEL (0323) 763212

THE PLOUGH AND HORSES

Walshes Road, Crowborough.
Tel: (0892) 652614

Hours: *Open for coffee, lunch and dinner, except Mon (last orders 9.45pm).*

Average Prices: *A la Carte £11; Sun lunch £7.95; bar meals from £1.25.*

Wines: *£4.25 per bottle; 90p per glass.*

Fresh-faced and pretty, off the beaten track down country lanes, yet a mere five minutes from the centre of Crowborough, David and Brenda Newton's fine inn, The Plough and Horses, is worth seeking out. A spacious, airy, 48-seat restaurant upstairs offers imaginative selections à la carte, with chicken breasts in white wine or chicken supreme; fresh fish, with trout meunière, scampi provençale and Dover sole, and a range of steaks. There are sirloins, fillets and T-bones, with recipes such as steak au poivre, tournedos sauté aux champignons (with mushrooms), tournedos Rossini, steak Diane, creole steak and steak chasseur. Both starters and desserts are varied and well chosen to complement the main courses. Such is the popularity, booking is advisable for dinner and Sunday lunch in particular. The options in the bar range from ploughman's lunches to steak sandwiches, home-made soup, salads, omelettes and chip meals. The Plough and Horses is to be found on the lower, back road from Jarvis Brook to Crowborough.

Tel: (0892) 652614

THE BLUE ANCHOR

Beacon Road, Crowborough.
Tel: (0892) 654519

Hours:	*Open for coffee, lunch and dinner (last orders 9.30pm).*
Average Prices:	*A la Carte £10.50; Sun lunch £5.95.*
Wines:	*From £5.10 per bottle.*

The wishing well in the photograph below, just a corner of the lovely gardens, may seem an odd aspect to show of this attractive inn. However, this is the inn which has won the Phoenix Brewery Beer Garden of the Year Award — one of the most prized and difficult awards to win. The patio and gardens (complete with an aviary and pet rabbits and goats) are as pretty as a picture, and there is an adventure play area for children. Furthermore, The Blue Anchor has won the Professional Publican award and has long been acknowledged as one of the finest food inns in Sussex, picking up a Quality Food accolade too. Daily specials are shown on the blackboard which offers seasonal game, fresh fish, home-made pies, casseroles, traditional roasts and puddings. With the menu fresh every day and variety assured, there is always plenty of choice. Sunday lunch is available at half-price for children under ten years old. Real ales are on draught at the bar. Visa, Access and American Express cards are welcomed and there is a large car park.

The Patio at the Blue Anchor, Crowborough. Tel: 0892 654519

THE HALF MOON

Friar's Gate, Crowborough.
Tel: (089 26) 61270

Hours: *Open for lunch and dinner, except Mon evenings (last orders 10.30pm).*

Average Prices: £3.50–£8.

Wines: *£4.75 per bottle; 90p per glass.*

The Half Moon at Friar's Gate is an inn of charm and character, set in a country lane at the edge of Ashdown Forest, near Crowborough. Featured on television, it is a 'fun' inn, run by young people, including its owner, Lady Arabella. The inn stands in its own unspoilt gardens, by a stream and shaded with trees, and is a haven for children, animals and all those who appreciate an English inn at its rural best. Salads and fruit concoctions abound, and the fare ranges from simple ploughman's lunches to vegetarian lasagne, leek croustade, devilled fresh crab and home-made steak and kidney pie. There are sandwiches and omelettes, a range of starters and satisfying desserts. The menu for dinner is always changing, but booking is advisable. Traditional roasts are served on Sundays and real ales are available at the bar. Live music adds to the attraction on Saturdays. If you do venture out to the garden to see the geese, goats, rabbits and bantams, watch out for the mean-looking ram (but we do understand that he's quite safe!).

THE HALF MOON
FRIARS GATE
CROWBOROUGH

Telephone: (08926) 61270

THE BOAR'S HEAD INN

Boar's Head, near Crowborough.
Tel: (0892) 652412

Hours: *Open 11am–2.30pm and 6–11pm, Mon–Fri,*
                   and 12–3pm and 7–10.30pm, Sun.

Average Prices: *Table d'Hôte £9.95/£11.95; Sun lunch £7.95.*

Wines: *From £4.95 per bottle; £1 per glass.*

Over 600 years old, The Boar's Head really does represent all that is good in an English inn, with its real log fires, real ales, low beams, sparkling glass and polished oak. Outside, the frontage is tile-hung; within, sporting prints and original paintings adorn the walls, along with two massive boars' heads, their imposing presence quite in contrast to the warmth of the welcome. To eat there are salads and sandwiches, ploughman's lunches and cold meat platters and the house special is the 'Boar's Bap', a freshly baked bap, filled with beef, ham, pâté, prawns or cheese. More substantially, the menu of home-cooked fare, for snacks or three course meals, includes dishes like steak and kidney pie, steaks, chicken, duckling, swordfish and other imaginative recipes. Gordon and Jill McKenzie are your hosts and it is their attention to detail, down to selecting the produce used in the kitchen, which has earned the popularity which this inn enjoys. There is plenty of parking and a lovely garden for use in fine weather.

Boar's Head, Crowborough.   *Tel: (0892) 652412*

MARK CROSS INN

Mark Cross, near Rotherfield.
Tel: (089 285) 2423

Hours: *Open 11am–11pm (restaurant 10pm) for coffee, lunch,*
tea and dinner. Sun 12–9.30pm.

Average Prices: £1–£12.

Wines: *House wine £3.20 per half-litre; £6.40 per litre.*

Another of Whitbread's Brewers Fayre establishments, the well-known Mark Cross Inn has plenty going for it. Lovely to look at, spacious and airy inside, beautifully appointed and professionally run, it also has pleasant gardens with sloping lawns and tables with umbrellas. Children can amuse themselves on the adventure games, and the inn enjoys the peace of the countryside whilst being just a ten minute drive from the centre of Tunbridge Wells and close to Wadhurst, Rotherfield and Mayfield. The menu offers all the popular dishes for which Brewers Fayre has become known, with a daily specials blackboard giving details of starters, two fish dishes, two meat dishes and a vegetarian dish. Regular choices range from appetisers, hot platters and fresh salads to light bites and desserts, all realistically priced. Mick and Chris Richardson supervise every aspect of the running of this inn where Visa and Access cards are accepted and there is a large car park.

THE MARK CROSS INN

MARK CROSS
NR. ROTHERFIELD
TEL: (089 285) 2423

THE NEVILL CREST AND GUN

Eridge Green, near Tunbridge Wells.
Tel: (0892) 864209

Hours: *Open for lunch and dinner (last orders 9.30pm).*
                        Bar meals lunchtime and evenings.

Average Prices: *£1–£8.50.*

Wines: *House wine from £3.20 per half-litre; £6.40 per litre.*

One of the loveliest and best known inns in this part of the county, The
Nevill Crest and Gun is now a Brewers Fayre establishment, offering the
quality of catering which has made Whitbread the leader in this field. The
Nevill, as it is called locally, stands in its own lovely gardens, set back from
the road, almost midway between Tunbridge Wells and Crowborough. In
line with Brewers Fayre tradition, there is everything from a simple
sandwich (open or closed, with a choice of brown or white bread, salad
garnish and relish, filled with roast beef, salmon, home-cooked ham,
English cheese or prawn) to a full four course repast. Pies, roasts, grills
and salads feature prominently. Attractive inside and out, The Nevill Crest
and Gun lends itself to parties, celebrations, intimate dinners and
lunchtime get-togethers. There is a large car park and Access and Visa
cards are welcomed. Close to Scotney Castle, Bayham Abbey, Penshurst
Place and other points of interest.

THE NEVILL CREST & GUN

ERIDGE GREEN, EAST SUSSEX.
TEL. (0892) 864209

BASSETTS RESTAURANT

37 High Street, Frant. Tel: (0892) 75635

Hours: *Open for lunch, Tues–Fri (reservations only), and dinner, Tues–Sat (last orders 9pm).*

Average Prices: *Fixed price menu £16.50.*

Wines: *From £6 per bottle.*

Long established and extremely popular, with one of the finest reputations in the entire county, Bassetts Restaurant enjoys one of the most picturesque settings too. In a village square, opposite an inn and in the shadow of the church, this cottage restaurant offers a menu which changes every three weeks to take fullest advantage of seasonal specialities from asparagus to loganberries, from pheasant to locally caught trout and from new potatoes to fresh garden peas. There is always something new and different to choose from, a result of this careful planning; starters such as escargots in wafer thin pastry with hazelnuts and herbs, pastry tartlet filled with mushrooms and quail eggs, and terrine of sweetbreads and pistachios exemplify this. Main courses may include breast of duckling with gooseberries, fresh salmon in filo pastry with herbs or breast of pheasant with clementines, and the dessert selection is equally imaginative. Over 80 fine wines are available and huge wine racks dominate the dining area, with its low, beamed ceiling and subtle lighting which adds to the comfort. The service, though unobtrusive, is friendly. Access and Visa cards welcomed.

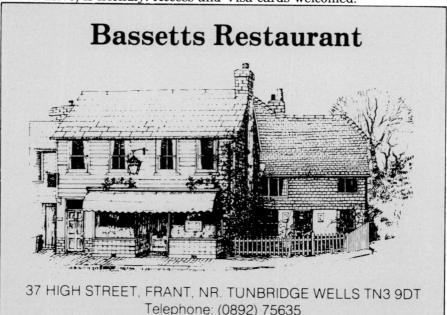

Bassetts Restaurant

37 HIGH STREET, FRANT, NR. TUNBRIDGE WELLS TN3 9DT
Telephone: (0892) 75635

THE ABERGAVENNY ARMS

Frant, near Tunbridge Wells.
Tel: (089 275) 233

Hours: *Open for lunch and dinner, except Mon evenings (last orders 9.30pm).*

Average Prices: *A la Carte £14; bar meals from £1.35.*

Wines: *From £5.25 per bottle.*

This fine 15th century inn is less than ten minutes' drive from the centre of Tunbridge Wells. Full of atmosphere and character, the inn is haunted by the ghost of a coachman who supposedly died on the premises. In those days an unexplained death caused panic and inns where this happened were closed. So they threw the body out into the courtyard to avoid closure, but, it is said, he is often heard trying to get in again! The hospitality is rather better these days. There is a self-service arrangement for lunch and bar meals, featuring salads and side dishes, casseroles and many popular traditional English dishes, providing everything from a simple ploughman's lunch to a four course meal. A new restaurant, seating 50, has been added since the last time The Aber'genny (as it is known locally) was included in *Where to Eat*. There are first class ales too, and friendly country-style hospitality. Booking is advisable at weekends; Access and Visa cards are welcome. The inn's name comes from the Marquis of Abergavenny who lives nearby in Eridge.

The
Abergabenny Arms

FRANT, TUNBRIDGE WELLS
Tel. (089 275) 233

THE OLD VINE

Cousley Wood, Wadhurst.
Tel: (089 288) 2271

Hours: *Open for lunch and dinner, except Sun evening.*
Average Prices: *A la Carte from £8.50.*
Wines: *£4.50 per bottle.*

One of the most popular inns in the county, The Old Vine at Cousley Wood had long been a great favourite, and it is for this reason that, despite the fact that the restaurant seats 90, it is essential to book for evening meals. In fact, on Monday evenings, when the highly regarded Denny Daniels Trio play, booking is sometimes needed several weeks in advance. The menu is constantly varied, but an indication of the kitchen's style can be gleaned from dishes like local pheasant in red wine with mushrooms, onions and chestnuts, freshly caught trout, saddle of Kentish lamb, veal Stroganoff, roast duckling and chicken Kiev, and there are always steaks too. Vegetables are fresh and, for a starter, the moules marinière are great local favourites (it is said that people come from Maidstone, Tonbridge, Tunbridge Wells and even Hastings for this house speciality). A good choice of desserts rounds off; there is a comprehensive wine list and vintage ports. Whitbread real ales are on draught in the bar. Access and Visa cards are welcomed.

THE OLD VINE, Cousley Wood, Wadhurst. Tel: (089 288) 2271

BEST BEECH HOTEL

Mayfield Lane, Best Beech, Wadhurst.
Tel: (089 288) 2046

Hours:	*Open for lunch and dinner (last orders 9.30pm).*
Average Prices:	*Set prices £8.95/£9.95/£11.25; bar meals from £1.*
Wines:	*From £4.50 per bottle.*

Long established and full of charm and character, the Best Beech is (and has all the friendliness of) an inn, although it is called an hotel. Low beamed ceilings run throughout, the one in the main bar boasting a particularly fine collection of mugs. The inn has a 26-seater restaurant which is cosy and warm and where home-cooked food is served. A la carte, there are three selections at fixed prices. At £8.95 choose from soup, pâté or prawn cocktail for starter, then escalope of veal Holstein, chicken Kiev, coq au vin or prawn salad for main course. There is a larger selection at £9.95 and, at £11.25, diners can choose from Mediterranean prawns in garlic, crab claws, mussels with garlic or smoked salmon (starters); T-bone steak, peppered sirloin, poached salmon, chicken Balmoral or beef Stroganoff. All three menus offer sweets from the trolley. The bar food ranges from traditional ploughman's lunches to turkey, ham and mushroom pie, chicken tandoori, steaks, oriental dishes, salads and other selections. There is a children's room and accommodation. Rhian and Dick Ansell are your hosts; Access and Visa cards.

The Best Beech Hotel   Telephone: (089 288) 2046

THE PRINCE OF WALES CARVERY RESTAURANT

Hailsham Road, Heathfield. Tel: (043 52) 2919

Hours: *Open for lunch and dinner.*

Average Prices: Carvery with dessert, coffee and mints £7.25.

The carvery at The Prince of Wales is one of the most popular free house restaurants in the county. Real ales, friendly and attentive staff and an attractive restaurant (seating over 50) are the main reasons for its popularity. Lunch offers roasts, pies, curries and the like from the hot buffet; evenings and Sundays have the carvery in full swing with ribs of beef, roast Sussex turkey, gammon, pork and other selections. Access and Visa cards welcome.

THE PRINCE OF WALES CARVERY RESTAURANT

HAILSHAM ROAD · HEATHFIELD
TEL: (043 52) 2919

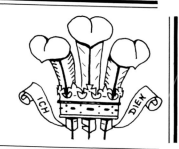

THE TUDOR HOUSE

High Street, Burwash. Tel: (0435) 882258

Hours: *Open for lunch, Wed–Fri and Sun in winter. Dinner Tues–Sat. Reservations advisable*

Average Prices: Fixed price £12.95; lunch/Sun lunch £8.50.

Wines: *From £5.50 per bottle; £1.15 per glass.*

The Tudor House is cosy, and full of character. Traditional English dishes are complemented by French and Italian specialities, and desserts include the old-fashioned favourites (all home-made). Comprehensive and reasonably priced wine list.The last Friday of each month is a special fish night.

The Tudor House Restaurant

High Street
Burwash   Tel: 0435 882258

THE BELL INN

High Street, Burwash. Tel: (0435) 882304

Hours: *Open for lunch and dinner, except Sun evenings (last orders 9.30pm).*

Average Prices: *A la Carte £9; bar meals from £1.20.*

Wines: *House wine from £4.65 per bottle; 90p per glass.*

The fine reputation for good food which this lovely inn enjoys is enhanced year after year. David Mizel and Annick Howard are great believers in real home-cooking, using only the best local produce, fresh fish and poultry' and properly hung meat and game. The restaurant itself seats 40, and there is plenty of room throughout the inn to enjoy meals in spacious comfort. This is a genuinely unspoilt inn; there are no jukeboxes and no one-armed bandits, but occasional folk music instead, much to the delight of local residents who remember The Bell as one of the best venues for folk. Mulled wine is served in winter when the glow of log fires offsets the dark oak beaming. Dishes include beef Wellington, carpetbagger steak (stuffed with oysters in a bordelaise sauce), lamb and mint kebabs, a seafood platter and home-baked pizzas. Nothing is bought ready-prepared or frozen, and desserts feature fresh pancakes, blackberry and apple pie, and an unusual strawberry and Drambuie shortcake, to mention but three. Coffee is freshly brewed and real ales are on draught at the bar.

The Middle House

Mayfield, East Sussex TN20 6AB
Tel: Mayfield (0435) 872146

THE MIDDLE HOUSE

Mayfield.
Tel: (0435) 872146

Hours: *Open for coffee, lunch, tea and dinner (last orders 10pm).*

Average Prices: *Table d'Hôte £16.95; Sun lunch £9.95; bar meals from £2.*

Wines: *House wine £5.95 per bottle; £7.50 per litre.*

Despite the fact that The Middle House is one of the finest examples of Elizabethan timbered architecture in the country, the prices reveal that it is not an expensive venue. Furthermore, the pleasant informality and friendliness of the hotel and restaurant are refreshingly relaxing. In many ways like one of the old traditional English market town hotels, The Middle House, with its huge inglenook fireplaces, dark oak beams and polished wood furniture, is a welcoming place of bustle and activity.

The hotel has eight bedrooms, all en suite and with the latest facilities, and the restaurant seats 55 in comfort. Here the menu changes every other day, but for some idea of the dishes to be found, the following are fairly typical. Start with smoked salmon and halibut terrine with a yoghurt and herb sauce, or perhaps duck breast pâté with toasted almonds and redcurrant sauce. There's an unusual savoury blue cheese roulade with a chilled tomato and herb sauce or a baked peach with cheese glaze and mango sauce, as further possibilities.

For main course the selections include dishes such as fillet of prime beef wrapped in bacon with Stilton and red wine sauce, and best end of lamb with a cherry tomato and spinach cream sauce. Grilled duck with passion fruit and stem ginger may be another option, or there may be monkfish with prawns, or game casserole with port and redcurrants, all providing a pleasantly different alternative to the often unimaginative menus of many hotels. Chocolate banana cheesecake hints at the thought which goes into the preparation of the many desserts.

Bar meals are similarly popular. Over 12 different ploughman's lunches are available, featuring Stilton, Brie, Danish Blue, Gorgonzola and other cheeses. Salad choices include poached or smoked salmon, or possibly seafood or roast meats (beef, pork and lamb). Steak, kidney and oyster pie is also on the menu, alongside baked trout and favourites like shepherd's pie, steaks and grills.

The gardens have amusements for the children and there is a large private car park. All leading credit cards — Access, Visa, American Express and Diner's Club — are welcomed.

THE THREE CUPS INN

Three Cups Corner, Punnetts Town, near Heathfield.
Tel: (0435) 830252

Hours: *Open for coffee, lunch and dinner (last orders 9pm).*
Average Prices: *A la Carte from £7.50; bar meals from £1.*
Wines: *From £5 per bottle; 95p per glass.*

Len and Renie Smith took over this most attractive country inn in November 1988. With dedication (and completely ignoring the resident ghost), they set about creating a truly traditional country inn, offering home-cooking, real ales, open wood fires and meticulously maintained gardens and meadows. Dating from the 1600s, much of the original character of The Three Cups has been maintained and the old oak beams, interesting pictures and cottagey atmosphere are part of the charm of the inn. But there is now a children's room (and a half-price menu for children), and in the bar the menu includes sandwiches, salads, ploughman's lunches and jacket potatoes (filled with cheese and onion, baked beans, cheese and ham and more). A la carte, the starters feature pâté and toast, and various home-made farmhouse soups which change with the seasons. For main course there are steaks, salads and fish (rainbow trout, for example, filled with celery, walnuts and crabmeat, served with an almond coating with parsley butter, salad and sauté potatoes). Registered with camping and caravan clubs.

The Three Cups Inn

Three Cups Corner, Punnetts Town, nr Heathfield. Tel: (0435) 830252

THE SMUGGLER'S WHEEL

Boreham Street, Herstmonceux. Tel: (0323) 832293

Hours: *Open for lunch and dinner, except Sun evening and Mon (last orders 9.30pm).*

Average Prices: *A la Carte from £11.50; Table d'Hôte £9.50; dinner £11.50.*

Wines: *From £6.75 per bottle.*

One of the loveliest restaurants in the county of Sussex, the 17th century, timbered farmhouse that is The Smuggler's Wheel has earned many accolades and awards for owners Giovanni and Nello Scamardella. Featured for many years now in *Where to Eat*, this restaurant's reputation grows and grows, making it essential to book in advance. One of the most interesting facets of The Smuggler's Wheel is that, whilst the menu is essentially authentic Italian in concept, it also features some very English dishes, including traditional steamed puddings (steamed in cloth, the old-fashioned way) and the great British roasts. Sunday lunch, for example, usually offers roast sirloin of beef, roast Kentish lamb and game in season. The wine list has some 60–70 selections, all personally chosen by Giovanni to be compatible with the considerable variety on the menu. A balcony overlooks well-tended gardens and there are excellent facilities for weddings, small conferences, private parties, directors' dining and other functions. All leading credit cards are accepted.

The Smuggler's Wheel

Tel: (0323) 832293

Boreham Street
Herstmonceux

THE HORSE SHOE INN

Windmill Hill, Herstmonceux.
Tel: (0323) 833265

Hours: *Open for lunch and dinner (last orders 10.30pm, 11pm Sat, 10pm Sun).*

Average Prices: *A la Carte £10.50; lunch from £2.75.*

Wines: *From £4.75 per bottle.*

This spacious and impressive inn is one of the Resort Hotels houses, displaying a Tudor-style black and white facade. With 15 bedrooms, all en suite and with the latest amenities, and excellent conference and functions facilities, The Horse Shoe Inn is a much sought-after venue for business executive and tourist alike. The restaurant here is The Baron of Beef and the menu presents an attractive selection of dishes from which to choose, à la carte, plus a daily table d'hôte menu. Six starters include a seafood creole and a home-made soup of the day; a variety of main courses gives a choice of sirloin, rump, fillet and T-bone steaks, steak au poivre, roast half-duckling, fillet of plaice and more. Salads are always available and desserts feature the popular Black Forest gâteau, blackcurrant cheesecake and pear neapolitan, alongside other temptations. The 16 special coffees are further enticements. All leading credit cards are welcomed. Large car park and pleasant grounds.

Horse Shoe *Inn*

Windmill Hill
Herstmonceux

Resort *Hotels*

Telephone: (0323) 833265
or Central Reservations Freephone: (0800) 500100

WALDERNHEATH COUNTRY RESTAURANT

Amberstone Corner, Hailsham. Tel: (0323) 840143

Hours:	*Open for coffee, lunch and dinner (last orders 9.30pm). Closed Sun evening and all day Mon.*
Average Prices:	*£1.50–£16.50; Sun lunch £11.75.*
Wines:	*From £6.50 per bottle.*

This lovely 15th century restaurant celebrated its 20th anniversary in 1989 and Paul and Ann Hill, the owners, are justifiably proud of their success. Certainly the Waldernheath is one of the most acclaimed restaurants in southern England and has a reputation for quality and variety. Chef-proprietor Paul studied and worked at many top hotels in Switzerland and Paris before opening the Waldernheath in the late 60's. Classical French cuisine has become his hallmark, although English traditional fare is also served, using fresh vegetables from the restaurant's own kitchen garden. Scottish beef is used for the roasts, steaks and the filet mignon; Sussex lamb, Gressingham duck and English game (in season) are employed for the many different recipes on a constantly changing, imaginative menu. The Waldernheath has a lovely patio where guests can eat al fresco when the weather is good, and, in winter, real blazing log fires. Booking is essential at this informal, friendly family-run restaurant set in a lovely country house with a cosy cottagey atmosphere. All leading credit cards are accepted. See also *Chef's Choice*.

Waldernheath Country Restaurant

High class French and traditional English cuisine

Amberstone Corner, Hailsham, East Sussex
Tel: Hailsham 840143

THE LAMB INN

Wartling, Herstmonceux.
Tel: (0323) 832116

Hours: *Open for dinner, Tues–Sat, and Sun lunch. Bar meals every lunchtime.*

Average Prices: *Carvery £9.50.*

Wines: *£4.75 per bottle; 90p per glass.*

The Lamb Inn, situated in the pretty little village of Wartling, just a few miles from Herstmonceux and Pevensey, is a lovely example of an English inn. A charming free house, owned by Pam and Bob Aylett, it has a fine reputation for food and is always lively and busy. Oak beams, log fires, a polished bar and gleaming brass and copper greet visitors when they arrive, and a pint of real ale quenches the thirst whilst the menu is surveyed. The highlight is the carvery, where the choice is between freshly roasted joints and poultry. There are usually three or four selections: beef, pork and lamb are always available and the fourth may be venison, turkey or pheasant, according to the season and the market selection. A fine range of fresh vegetables and salads accompanies, and desserts are served at the table, followed by coffee and mints. Lunchtime sees a menu of daily specials and other choices, from ploughman's lunches to scampi, salads and steak and kidney pie. A pleasant garden and ample parking are two further attributes.

THE LAMB INN

Wartling, Nr. Herstmonceux
Tel: (0323) 832116

THE RED LION

Hooe, near Battle.
Tel: (0424) 892371

Hours: *Open for coffee and bar meals, 12–2pm and 6–8.45pm.*
                  Snacks only Sat evening and Sun.
Average Prices: *Snacks and meals from 90p.*
Wines: *From £4.50 per bottle.*

This inn has been in the same family for over 70 years, and now Ruth and Keith Barton run one of the most popular hostelries in the county. Over 500 years old, The Red Lion is a fine example of an English country inn; it has real ales and home-cooked, unpretentious food at reasonable prices. The ploughman's lunch is a hunk of freshly-baked bread with real cheese and pickle, and then there are ham, egg and chips; steak and kidney pie; fish and a variety of salads, including fresh crab, beef, cheese and more. There are toasted sandwiches, seafood platters (with plaice, codling, haddock, scampi, etc.), gammon rashers and hamburgers. Once the haunt of smugglers, The Red Lion really does have a ghost, that of a phantom snuff-grinder, and has featured in several books about the supernatural. It's also a rendezvous for motor enthusiasts and has a collection of rare motoring memorabilia on the walls. There is a fine children's play area, tables in the garden, car parking and, in winter, blazing log fires. One of the most hospitable inns in Sussex.

COODEN RESORT HOTEL

Cooden Beach, Bexhill-on-Sea.
Tel: (042 43) 2281

Hours:	*Open for coffee, lunch, tea and dinner (last orders 9.30pm). Bar meals in the Sovereign Tavern.*
Average Prices:	*Table d'Hôte £15; Sun lunch (carvery) £12; bar meals from £3.50.*
Wines:	*From £7.50 per bottle.*

A member of the renowned Resort Hotels group, the Cooden Resort Hotel has long been one of the most elegant and attractive hotels in the South. With a 120-seat restaurant and a separate 80-seat grill room restaurant, it has everything to offer, being an ideal venue for every type of function, from business conferences to private parties and subtly-lit tête-à-tête dinners. The à la carte selection of dishes varies with the seasons, also taking into account the day's catch. Chef Paul Fermor has been with the hotel for 22 years and is equally at home with a society banquet as with the daily luncheon menu — the same imaginative approach applies. To complete the hotel picture, there are 36 luxury bedrooms and a complete health club where guests can work up an appetite in the heated swimming pool or in the sauna and solarium. The Cooden Resort Hotel stands right on the beach; the sea is less than 50 yards from the hotel and the lawns stretch almost to the water's edge.

COODEN RESORT HOTEL

Cooden Beach, Bexhill-on-Sea, East Sussex. Tel: (04243) 2281

Resort Hotels PLC

LYCHGATES RESTAURANT

Church Street, Old Town, Bexhill-on-Sea.
Tel: (0424) 212193

Hours: *Open for lunch, Tues–Fri, and dinner, Tues–Sat from 7.15pm.*

Average Prices: *Fixed price menus: lunch £7.95; dinner £12.50 (3 courses), £14.95 (5 courses).*

Wines: *From £6.75 per bottle.*

This highly-regarded restaurant has now been open for three years. It is owned and run by John Tyson and his wife, Sue. With a childhood ambition to be a chef, John aimed high. At the age of nine he declared his intention to be a chef at London's famed Dorchester Hotel. Not only did he achieve this aim, but also went on to cater for royalty, 10 Downing Street and Lord Mayors' banquets. The collection of his menus which decorate the walls of Lychgates tell part of the story. Here his menus change monthly, though an indication of his flair can be seen in dishes like Belgian endive with a purée of chicken and pistachio nuts, to be found amongst the starters. A platter of smoked fish may follow, and then a palate-cleansing home-made sorbet before a main course such as medallions of venison with blackcurrant and liquorice, or quenelles of sea bass and turbot. The value for money in the fixed price menus is remarkable. Access and Visa cards are accepted.

Lychgates Restaurant

Church Street,
Old Town,
Bexhill-on-Sea
East Sussex
TN40 2HE
Tel: (0424) 212193

THE MIRAMAR

De La Warr Parade, Bexhill-on-Sea.
Tel: (0424) 220360

Hours: *Open for breakfast, coffee, lunch and tea (10.30am–5.30pm Wed–Sun in summer, 10.30am–4.30pm Fri–Sun in winter).*

Average Prices: Snacks and meals from 95p.

Under the same ownership as the well known Corianders restaurant, also in Bexhill, The Miramar is a restaurant with a difference. The same insistence upon fresh produce is still adhered to, but the menu is far more extensive in scope. There are favourite dishes which include coq au vin, harvest chicken, Sussex hot pot, fisherman's pie, Grandma's sausage pie and steak and kidney, beef and tomato, and pork and pineapple hot pots; there are mixed grills, salads, sandwiches, country snacks and savouries, pasta dishes and a selection of ploughman's lunches and toasted sandwiches. There are children's choices too, and one of the finest dessert selections to be found in the county, offering real dairy ice creams, Sussex apple pies, sundaes, fudge cakes and house specials such as Sorbet Surprise, Miramar Banana Delight and Pavlova Miramar. Situated right on the seafront in the quieter part of town, The Miramar, although unlicensed, is a great change from the usual seaside restaurant. It also has two flats to let throughout the year.

Home-cooked meals
MORNING COFFEE
Afternoon **Tea COUNTRY BRUNCH**
FULL MENU SERVED ALL DAY

MIRAMAR

A country treat on Bexhill seafront
De la Warr Parade (Nr. Galley Hill) Bexhill 220360

CORIANDERS

66 Devonshire Road, Bexhill-on-Sea.
Tel: (0424) 220329

Hours: *Open for coffee, lunch and tea. Dinner on Fri/Sat evenings (last orders 8.30pm).*

Average Prices: *Meals and snacks 50p–£5.*

Wines: *Licensed for wines and real ales.*

Time was when vegetarians were often thought of as cranks. Now it is realised that wholefoods, organically grown products and healthy eating in general make good sense. Corianders is not just a vegetarian restaurant, however, far from it; everything is fresh, home-made and natural, right down to fresh fruit juices, freshly ground coffee, fresh yoghurts and organically produced wines. To eat there is a fine selection of interesting dishes: flans and quiches, salads and hot pots, and a vegetable curry. Bread is freshly baked, as are scones and cakes, and one of the specialities is the real dairy ice cream, a world away from ordinary (and mis-named) commercial ice cream. To accompany meals there are real ales and Merrydown fruit wines. On Friday and Saturday evenings an entirely different menu is served, with waitress service of an à la carte selection of dishes, whilst, in summer months, the open-air tea garden is particularly pleasant. Ken and Carolyn Simmons are the proprietors and their enthusiasm is evident throughout.

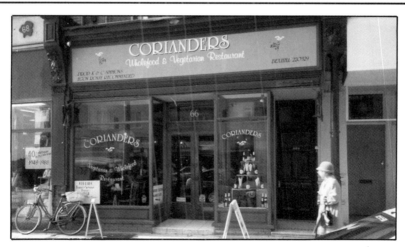

CORIANDERS
Wholefood & vegetarian restaurant

66, Devonshire Road, Bexhill-on-Sea. Tel: (0424) 220329
EGON RONAY RECOMMENDED

THE DENBIGH

Little Common Road, Bexhill-on-Sea.
Tel: (0424) 33817

Hours: *Open for coffee, lunch and dinner (last orders 10pm).*
Bar meals lunchtime and evening.

Average Prices: *A la Carte from £7.50; bar meals from £2.*

Wines: *House wine £6.40 per litre; £3.30 per half-litre.*

One of the liveliest inns in the Bexhill area with its special event nights, the live entertainment and the landlord's singalong evenings. A pretty inn, it stands midway between Bexhill and Little Common, on the Eastbourne road, and is a popular venue for those who enjoy the atmosphere of a country inn and an extensive menu choice, in addition to the fun occasions. The lunchtime selection of dishes spans ten starters, from corn-on-the-cob and pâté to smoked mackerel, whilst for main course the fresh, home-made dishes include steak and kidney (or mushroom) pie, cottage pie, cauliflower cheese, vegetable lasagne and ratatouille. The hefty mixed grill is one of the favourites, offered as an alternative to 8oz rump and fillet steaks; but on Friday evenings on 8oz rump steak dinner for two costs only £7.95. Bar meal-wise, locally-caught fish, chicken Kiev, venison in red wine, salads and more steaks vie for prominence with daily specials. Barbecues are held outside in the country garden on Sundays in summer. Real ales accompany and there is plenty of car parking.

The Denbigh *Little Common Road, Bexhill-on-Sea*

LA CUISINE

11 Grand Parade, St Leonards-on-Sea.
Tel: (0424) 437589

Hours: *Open for lunch and dinner, except Tues.*

Average Prices: *Lunch from £4.50 (2 courses); dinner £11.50/£13.50*
(4 courses); Sun lunch £7.95.

Wines: *From £6.55 per bottle.*

La Cuisine is a restaurant with a fine reputation in a delightful location. The Continental/English menu at La Cuisine is a welcome find. Dinner à la carte has starters such as genuine pâté de foie gras truffée from Strasbourg, and Russian caviar, served with Russian pancakes and iced vodka. Main courses include sea bass, fresh lobster and a rich variety of fresh fish and shellfish, plus specialities de la maison such as magret de canard glacé au miel et jus aux cinque poivres, medallions of beef en croûte and filet de boeuf tartare. The menu is in French, but there is English translation and, as the menu truly reflects the style of cooking mastered by chef John C Day, there is nothing pretentious about this restaurant. Menus change with the seasons, so dishes quoted are merely examples, and at Christmas, in particular, La Cuisine is very lively, with bookings for the festive period required weeks in advance. The occasional special gourmet evenings include live entertainment. Access and Visa cards are welcomed.

11 Grand Parade, St Leonards-on-Sea. Tel: (0424) 437589

RÖSERS

64 Eversfield Place, St Leonards-on-Sea.
Tel: (0424) 712218
Hours: *Open for lunch and dinner except Sat lunchtime. Closed*
Sun (last orders 10.30pm).
Average Prices: *A la Carte £16–£24.*
Wines: *From £6 per bottle.*

Recipient of many accolades, Rösers of Hastings is one of the county's famous restaurants. A member of the Society of Master Chefs, Gerald Röser trained in Germany and Switzerland, and his reputation for culinary skill is widespread. The style is what is described as 'cuisine vivante' — a method using only the freshest of produce, influenced by the French nouvelle, but more inventive and imaginative and certainly more lavish, involving a careful selection of dishes which are particularly complementary to one another. Fresh seafood is the speciality of Rösers, and the dish 'Fantasy of Seafood' uses no less than seven or eight different fish and shellfish, including sea bass, turbot, salmon, king prawns and scallops. Scallops, again, sautéed in butter and served in a saffron sauce with Pernod, mangetout and a hint of garlic, is another popular creation. Rack of Romney Marsh lamb, with a crisp herbal crust shows variety. A cellar of over 300 wines includes classic vintages. Booking is essential.

Pelham Place, Hastings.

THE HARROW INN

828 The Ridge, Baldslow, St Leonards-on-Sea.
Tel: (0424) 751109

Hours: *Open for lunch and dinner (last orders 10pm).*
Bar meals at all times.

Average Prices: £1–£8.50.

Wines: *House wine from £3.20 per half-litre, £6.40 per litre.*

High on The Ridge, on the A2100 at the A21 junction, The Harrow is easy to find if you know where to look, and it is worth finding. The address of St Leonards is misleading; Baldslow is well before you drop down to St Leonards and the A2100 is the top road between Battle and Ore. A fine Brewers Fayre house, The Harrow is a most popular venue for business lunches, evenings out with friends, private parties or quick snacks. The dining room is spacious and airy and there is a lovely conservatory in which to enjoy your meal. Brewers Fayre quality is seen in the light bites, fresh salads and hot platters like steak and kidney pie (home-cooked steak and kidney topped with a light, crispy pastry, served with garden peas and carrots). Chicken with sage and onion stuffing is available at £3.50, for example, and this includes vegetables (all hot platters are served with french fried or other potatoes, plus a selection from the relish tray). Access and Visa cards are welcomed and there is ample car parking.

THE
HARROW
INN

828 THE RIDGE
BALDSLOW
ST. LEONARDS-ON-SEA

☎
(0424) 751109

PORTERS WINE BAR

56 High Street, Hastings. Tel: (0424) 427000

Hours: *Open 12–3pm and 7–11pm. Lunch 12–2pm and dinner 7–10pm. Closed Sun lunchtime.*

Average Prices: £1.35–£7.

Wines: *House wine from £4.60 per bottle.*

Different, interesting and most attractive, Porters Wine Bar is in the lovely Old Town part of Hastings, where the High Street is narrow and full of fascinating little shops and houses. Porters is on three levels, with a delightful secluded, tabled garden at the back where guests can eat al fresco. There is live music — a pianist — on Tuesday, Wednesday and Friday evenings — and the atmosphere is reminiscent of the relaxed pre-war years. The menu changes every day, but anything from a snack to a three course meal is available. For starters there may be dishes like mushrooms in cream and tarragon, pork pâté with French bread or deep-fried Brie with cranberry sauce. Main courses could include the popular beef and Guinness pie (served with red cabbage), goujons of plaice with garlic mayonnaise, smoked cod and leek gratin or chicken Kiev. There are side salads and garlic bread, home-made soups, Greek salads and venison sausages, all accompanied by one of the most comprehensive wine lists in Hastings. Visa and Access cards are welcomed.

PORTERS wine bar

56 High Street
Hastings

Tel: (0424) 427000

THE HOLLINGTON OAK

Wishing Tree Road, St Leonards-on-Sea.
Tel: (0424) 424104

Hours: *Open 11am–11pm, 12–10.30pm Sun. Lunch and dinner (last orders 10pm).*

Average Prices: *A la Carte £9; bar meals from £1.10.*

Wines: *From £5.95 per bottle.*

One of the finest inns in the county, The Hollington Oak, one of Whitbread's best, is hidden in a quiet road. Taking the road from St Leonards to Battle, and then the 'To Superstore' turn-off, The Hollington Oak is in Wishing Tree Road. It has long featured in *Where to Eat* and since the last edition has added a fully-equipped children's play area, with swings, slides, climbing frames and springy animals to keep them amused whilst adults enjoy the home-cooking for which the inn is known. Everything is fresh; local produce is used wherever possible, supervised by Angela Marshall, who runs the inn. Daily special main courses feature traditional roasts and grills, with steaks, chops, gammon and mixed grills, and there is a fine cold carvery offering turkey, beef and ham, together with a range of salads and side dishes. Private parties are welcome and, whilst this is an extremely popular and busy lunch venue, it is also a pleasant setting for a special celebration or a relaxed dinner. All leading credit cards are accepted.

THE HOLLINGTON OAK   Wishing Tree Road, St. Leonards-on-Sea

THE BEAUPORT PARK HOTEL

Battle Road, Hastings. Tel: (0424) 51222

Hours:	*Open for coffee, lunch, tea and dinner (last orders 9.30pm, 10pm Sat).*
Average Prices:	*A la Carte £14–£18; Table d'Hôte £12; light meals from £1.60.*
Wines:	*From £6 per bottle.*

The stately Beauport Park Hotel is set high above Hastings and stands in 30 acres of landscaped gardens, with a semi-formal walled garden and an outdoor swimming pool. The hotel has 23 en suite bedrooms, appointed to the highest standard with every convenience; for the diner, meanwhile, the meals are strongly French in concept, utilising the best English game, meat and poultry, especially fresh fish from the Hastings fleet. As a result, guests are able to enjoy sole bonne femme, deep-sea shark provencale, coquilles St Jacques Singapore, escalope of veal Marsala and other similarly imaginative dishes à la carte. On the table d'hôte dinner menu there may be a cream of turkey and mushroom soup or avocado and kiwi fruit salad, followed by a mixed grill or pan-fried chicken in a brandy and honey sauce, with a selection of cheeses or desserts to conclude. Light meals offered can include coquille fruits de mer, pâté en terrine or crêpes jardinière, and cream teas are served 2–6pm. All leading credit cards are accepted.

BEAUPORT PARK HOTEL

Battle Road, Hastings. Tel (0424) 51222

THE KING'S ARMS

Bexhill Road, Ninfield, near Battle.
Tel: (0424) 892263

Hours: *Open 11am–11pm for coffee, lunch, tea and dinner*
(last orders 10pm, 9.30pm Sun).

Average Prices: £1–£10.

Wines: *House wine from £6.40 per bottle (litre).*

The King's Arms is one of Whitbread's famed Brewers Fayre establishments. Transformed quite recently from an already spacious and attractive inn, this old coaching inn, on the Bexhill to London route, has been tastefully modernised, with facilities incorporated to accommodate almost every need. The restaurant seats 70, but the inn can cater for over 100 and is already extremely popular. Some of this popularity is due to the fact that, although the restaurant aspect is the primary service of the inn, it is still very much a pub, and the informal atmosphere encouraged by Tony and Dianne Pearson plays its part. The Brewers Fayre reputation for value can be seen in starters like hot mushrooms, farmhouse pâté and prawn cocktail, and then hot platters such as steak and kidney pie, 8oz gammon steaks, roast half-chicken, sirloin steak and fillet of plaice, all served with the attention to detail synonymous with this group. Furthermore, daily specials are displayed on the blackboard. Access and Visa cards are welcomed and there is a large car park.

THE KINGS ARMS

Bexhill Road
Ninfield
Nr Battle
Tel: (0424) 892263

THE UNITED FRIENDS

The Green, Ninfield, near Battle.
Tel: (0424) 892462

Hours: *Open for coffee, lunch and dinner (last orders 9.30pm).*
                     No food Mondays.

Average Prices: *A la Carte £11; bar snacks from £1.10.*

Wines: *From £4.90 per bottle; 90p per glass.*

The United Friends seems such an appropriate name for this popular little inn where the warmth of the welcome extended by hostess Eileen Hayden has made it a firm favourite. The restaurant seats 36 diners and the inn is known for its home-cooking in the traditional English style. Starters include prawn cocktail, egg mayonnaise, whitebait, pâté garni and soup, with, to follow, salmon steaks, scampi, pan-fried plaice, steak and kidney pie or T-bone and rump steaks. Alternatively, the selection of fresh salads extends from beef and chicken to prawn and mixed cold cuts. Desserts feature gâteaux, Dutch apple flan and similar, and cheese and biscuits are always available. For children — who are very welcome — there's a specially priced children's platter, offering fish fingers, sausages, etc. Harvey's and Shepherd Neame real ales are on draught and the inn has facilities for private functions and parties. Six en suite bedrooms accommodate those wishing to stay a little longer. Access and Visa cards are welcomed.

The United Friends

The Green, Ninfield, nr Battle. ☎ *(0424) 892462*

MOOR HALL HOTEL

Ninfield, Battle. Tel: (0424) 892330

Hours:	*Open for coffee, lunch, tea and dinner (last orders 9.30pm).*
Average Prices:	*A la Carte from £14; Table d'Hôte from £10.95; Sun lunch £10.95.*
Wines:	*From £5 per bottle; 90p per glass.*

Formerly an old country house, Moor Hall Hotel has been completely refurbished to create a luxury 25 room hotel. Standing in over 30 acres of gardens and woodland, it is an ideal venue for weddings, parties and conferences or for lunch and dinner. With facilities for buffets of up to 200 people and a separate dining room for up to 12 (well-suited for directors' meetings/lunches/dinners), the hotel also has a comfortable restaurant which seats 25 guests. Here the menu changes from day to day to use the best seasonal fare, but the thought which goes into the menus can be seen in starters such as smoked duck salad, watercress soup, strawberry and kiwi fruit salad, smoked chicken and dandelion with sorrel salad and fan of avocado with prawns. The main course to follow has included red mullet with lime and shallot sauce, roast turkey with chipolata and cranberry sauce, new season lamb with mint sauce and pan-fried sirloin steak with green peppercorn sauce. A highlight amongst the desserts is the three tier Bavarian cream. All leading credit cards are accepted.

MOOR HALL · *NINFIELD* · *BATTLE* · ☎ *0424 892330*

THE ROYAL OAK

Whatlington, near Battle.
Tel: (042 487) 492

Hours:	*Open for lunch and dinner (last orders 10pm).*
Average Prices:	*£5.50–£10.*
Wines:	*From £5 per bottle.*

The picture of this inn says it all. Although taken in the winter it shows just what a pretty place it is. Owner Tony Cronin is a butcher and his steaks are of the finest Scottish beef. Pies are made with beef selected at Ashford market by Tony himself. He says simply "This is a damn fine pub with really good, straightforward, no-nonsense real food"! Daily specials feature on the blackboard and well-kept real ales are on draught at the bar. An 80-foot well, with some 40-foot depth of water, inside the inn is a fascinating feature. Underwater passages lead off and this was once a smugglers' rendezvous — just part of The Royal Oak's interesting history. A visit will reveal more. See also the inside front cover of this book.

The Royal Oak, Whatlington, Nr. Battle.

THE SENLAC HOTEL

Lower Lake, Battle.
Tel: (042 46) 2034

Hours:	*Open for coffee, lunch and dinner (last orders 10pm).*
Average Prices:	*A la Carte from £5; bar meals from £1.50.*
Wines:	*From £5 per bottle.*

Historic Battle has much to see, do and enjoy, and one of the best-known refreshment spots in the area is The Senlac Hotel. In both the bar and the restaurant the choice of fare has made the inn one of the town's favourite rendezvous, where guests can savour anything from a ploughman's lunch (with the option of Cheddar, Stilton, smoked mackerel, ham and pâté) to a full four course repast, chosen à la carte. A blackboard displays the daily specials and these frequently feature the best of the day's catch at Hastings. In addition, there are prime steaks (a sirloin for around £7), fresh trout with almonds and classic dishes like beef Stroganoff and chicken Kiev, all realistically priced. A wide selection of sandwiches caters for the peckish, and there are ice creams, sorbets or The Senlac cheeseboard to finish, with freshly-made filter coffee completing the meal. Whitbread beers are served at the bar.

the
Senlac
Hotel

Battle - 04246·2034

THE BLACKSMITH'S RESTAURANT

43 High Street, Battle. Tel: (042 46) 3200

Hours: *Open for lunch and dinner (last orders 10.30pm).*
                    Closed all day Mon and Sun evenings in winter.

Average Prices: A la Carte £14; lunch £5.35 (2 courses); Sun lunch £8.90.

Wines: *£3.95 per half-litre; from £6.45 per bottle.*

By far the longest established restaurant in Battle, The Blacksmith's Restaurant is under the management of chef-proprietor Martin Howe, a member of the Institute of Master Chefs. The menu is one of international scope, combining British fare with French flair. However, Martin specialises in Hungarian cooking and, therefore, the variety of dishes on the frequently changed menu is great. There's value for money too; for £5.35 at lunchtime guests can choose from four starters, such as home-made soup or pâté, whitebait or egg mayonnaise, followed by fish of the day or a traditional roast of the day with all the trimmings. A la carte, the choice is wide, with house specialities including honey-roast duckling (crispy-coated and served with a home-made black cherry sauce) and fillet of beef Café de Paris (cooked in butter and served with a brandy and cream sauce). A highlight, though, is the authentic Hungarian goulash served with egg dumplings. Access, Visa and Diner's Club cards are accepted.

Diners Club International

43 High Street, BATTLE, East Sussex.
Telephone: Battle (042 46) 3200

THE ASH TREE

Brown Bread Street, Ashburnham, near Battle.
Tel: (0424) 892104

Hours:	*Open for lunch and dinner, except Mon.*
Average Prices:	*A la Carte/Table d'Hôte £8.95; lunch £1–£5.*
Wines:	*From £4.50 per bottle.*

When you find an inn which is as hidden away as this one, and yet is as busy and lively as a village centre pub, it must have something going for it. At The Ash Tree it is a mix of three things. First of all the reputation of the food has been built up through many years of obsession with quality and freshness by owner Janice Wellman. Secondly, The Ash Tree is an inn which has escaped the ravages of time, remaining truly unspoilt; dogs bask in front of the log fire, real ales are on draught and the atmosphere insists that you relax and take your ease. The third ingredient perhaps is that the inn is a 'discovery'. Known locally as 'The Little Lost Pub in the Woods', it really is tricky to find, though all the more worthwhile for that. There's no blaring jukebox, this is just a friendly, comfortable and pleasant inn which serves an à la carte selection of reasonably priced dishes ranging from seven starters to main courses like steaks, venison, rainbow trout, kebabs and more. Booking is advisable for dinner. Brandy is unusually served from old wooden barrels.

The Ash Tree Inn

Table d'hôte
A la Carte,
Lunchtimes
& evenings

Old English Meals
in
Old English
Settings

Brown Bread Street, Ashburnham, Nr. Battle, East Sussex. Tel: (0424) 892104

NETHERFIELD PLACE

Netherfield, near Battle. Tel: (042 46) 4455

Hours: *Open for coffee, lunch, tea and dinner (last orders 9.30pm).*

Average Prices: A la Carte £16; Sun lunch £11.50. Children half price.

Wines: *From £6.95 per bottle.*

In an exquisite setting, this gracious country house stands in 30 acres of parkland just two miles from Battle. The 12 luxurious bedrooms all have bathrooms en suite. The hotel's own acre and a half garden supplies much of the fresh produce, including the figs, grapes, strawberries and mushrooms and the restaurant has now added a special 'Inclusive Executive Luncheon' menu. The à la carte selection offers three home-made chef's soups — bouillabaisse Côte d'Azur, potage Parmentier, and velouté de Stilton Tradition — which is an old English cream of Stilton soup garnished with apple and celery. Eight hors d'oeuvre provide great variety and the main courses range from Dutch calves' liver, venison, Scotch fillet of beef, saddle of lamb and fresh quails to turbot filled with crab, fresh trout and Scottish salmon. All credit cards welcome. One of the best wine selections in the south of England.

Netherfield, Nr. Battle, Sussex. Tel: (04246) 4455

HOLMES HOUSE RESTAURANT

Sedlescombe, near Battle.
Tel: (042 487) 450

Hours: *Open for lunch and dinner, except Sat lunchtimes, Sun evening and Mon.*

Average Prices: *A la Carte from £15.50.*

Wines: *From £6.60 per bottle.*

One of the longest established restaurants in the county, Holmes House at Sedlescombe is also one of the most highly esteemed dining places. Full of character, with a first class reputation, it is run by Frank and Margaret Fleischer. The restaurant has been noted by all the leading critics at one time or another, and has even made the national press, none of which has adversely affected its proprietors or their welcome. It is a 15th century beamed cottage, with lovely gardens and a swimming pool where guests can enjoy themselves on occasion. Many come to lunch and stay all afternoon by the pool, finishing with dinner in the evening. The thoughtfully prepared menu offers fresh fish from Hastings, whole Dover sole, Scotch salmon, roast rack of Sussex lamb, escalope of veal, roast duckling, beef steak and mushroom pudding and more. Daily specials have featured fresh local lobster, cold with salad or thermidor, and the atmosphere is always hospitable.

Sedlescombe, Nr. Battle. Tel: (042 487) 450

THE SMUGGLER

Pett Level, near Hastings.
Tel: (0424) 813491

Hours: *Open for lunch and dinner, except Sun evening (last orders 9.45pm).*

Average Prices: *A la Carte £11; bar meals from £2.50.*

Wines: *House wine £5.25 per bottle (white); £5.45 per bottle (red).*

When visiting the Winchelsea area, Fairlight or points between Hastings and Rye, this is a most convenient inn. Right on the beach, with the sound of surf and seagulls, The Smuggler specialises in food and hospitality. Attractive in summer and buzzing with festivity in the Christmas season, the fare at this inn is home-cooked and features fresh fish — the best of the day's catch — all year round. In addition, there is a choice of steaks, cottage pie, liver and bacon and similar specialities, as well as a selection of ploughman's lunches, from Stilton and Cheddar to prawn and quiche. The blackboard displays the daily specials and real ales are on draught at the bar. The house wines too are of a high quality and are available by the carafe and by the bottle. Under the personal supervision of Barbara and Graham Cooper, The Smuggler is a free house which is ideally placed for spotting the wildfowl and seabirds for which this area is famed, and for exploring miles of unspoilt shoreline.

The Smuggler
FREE HOUSE

Pett Level, Nr. Hastings,
East Sussex

Telephone: 813491

BROOMHILL LODGE HOTEL AND RESTAURANT

Rye Foreign, Rye.
Tel: (079 78) 421

Hours: *Open for coffee, lunch, tea and dinner (last orders 9.30pm).*

Average Prices: *A la Carte £15; Table d'Hôte £8.50; Sun lunch £7.50.*

Wines: *From £5.75 per bottle.*

Now under entirely new management, this hospitable country hotel and restaurant has become even more attractive. Set high on a hill, a mile and a half from the centre of Rye, on the A268, Broomhill Lodge has 12 elegant and comfortable bedrooms, all with full facilities, and is ideally placed as a base for exploring the Romney Marshes, the ancient Cinque Port town of Rye and other places of interest. Broomhill also has a restaurant where the emphasis is placed firmly on locally produced fruit and vegetables, Rye Bay fish (fresh each day) and seasonal game and poultry. The dinner menu offers some five starters, including a game pâté and fresh sardines with walnut oil. There are six main courses, constantly changing but exemplified by dishes like roast duckling with apple sauce, pork escalope Holstein, fried lamb cutlets with tarragon, rainbow trout and rump steak with a pepper sauce, all rounded off by the chef's home-made desserts or a selection from the cheeseboard. Morning coffee and afternoon tea are also served. Visa and Access cards are welcomed.

BROOMHILL LODGE HOTEL & RESTAURANT

RYE FOREIGN,
RYE,
EAST SUSSEX

tel: (079 78) 421

RUMPELS INN AND MOTEL

Rye Road, Rye Foreign, Rye.
Tel: (079 721) 494

Hours:	*Open for coffee, lunch and dinner (last orders 9.30pm).*
Average Prices:	*A la Carte £10; Sun lunch £6.50; bar meals from £1.*
Wines:	*From £5 per bottle.*

One of the liveliest places around, Rumpels is an inn, a motel, a live music venue and a restaurant with a dance floor. Buffet facilities are available for up to 120 guests, private parties are welcomed by arrangement, and the children can enjoy the special play area with its own pets corner, complete with tame goats, rabbits, guinea fowl and lambs to entertain them. Bar meals are served and include curries, beefburgers, spaghetti, scampi and chip meals, as well as sandwiches, ploughman's lunches and salads. The restaurant menu, à la carte, offers starters such as Rumpels ribs (barbecued), mushrooms provençale, whitebait and buttered prawns. For main course, steak Diane is a great favourite, as is fillet steak Katrina (filled with prawns in a sauce of crushed peppercorns, mushrooms, tomato, onion, cream and garlic). The varied live music is on Fridays and Saturdays, and Rumpels has plenty of parking space and a large garden. The motel features 13 units, five in an unusual family suite, and the ancient town of Rye is but a short drive away. Access, Visa, American Express and Diner's Club cards are accepted.

Rye Road
Rye Foreign, Rye
Tel: (079 721) 494

THE TOP O'THE HILL AT RYE

Rye Hill, Rye.
Tel: (0797) 223284

Hours:	*Open for coffee, lunch and dinner (last orders 9.30pm).*
	Bar meals lunchtimes and evenings.

Average Prices: £1.50–£10.

Wines: *From £5 per bottle.*

The very appearance of The Top O'The Hill prepares you for what is to be found inside. It is crisp and clean, warmed by soft colourings and is family owned and run. High on the hill, as its name reflects, overlooking ancient Rye, this inn enjoys a first class reputation for its varied and imaginative cuisine. In addition to the regular menu, there are special vegetarian and children's dishes, but the scope of the kitchen is well illustrated by the standard choices alone. Eight starters range from home-made soup with granary bread to garlic mushrooms with cream, and from smoked salmon to Mexican pancakes. No less than five fresh fish dishes are offered for main course, and there are steaks, salads and over a dozen other options such as a popular coq au vin, game pie (when possible), steak and kidney pie and roast Kentish lamb with garden mint sauce. Real ales are available from the bar or there is a fine choice of wines. Bonuses include a pleasant garden with picnic tables, ample parking and accommodation. Access and Visa cards are welcomed.

Peter & Hazel Haydon
welcome you to

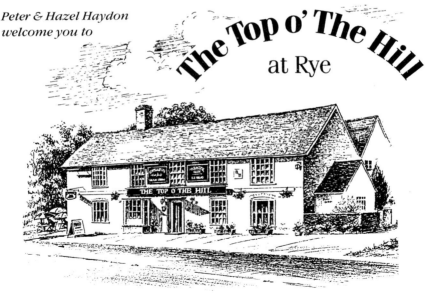

Rye Hill, East Sussex   Telephone: Rye (0797) 223284

THE GEORGE HOTEL

High Street, Rye.
Tel: (0797) 222114

Hours: *Open for coffee, lunch, tea and dinner (last orders*
                     9pm). Bar meals, except Sun.

Average Prices: *Lunch and dinner from £7.95; bar meals from £1.50.*

Wines: *From £6.95 per bottle.*

Set in the centre of this ancient town's quaint High Street, the 14th century George Hotel, a Trusthouse Forte establishment, is very much part of the charm and history of Rye. With 22 en suite bedrooms, complete with all modern facilities, and a spacious and impressive banqueting room, The George is always among the first hotels considered for business functions, weddings and other receptions. Bar meals are served in the charismatic John Crouch bar (named after a 17th century landlord), or there is lunch or dinner in the restaurant which offers a wide choice of fare at competitive prices. Sound, traditional English food is at the core of the menus, with strong emphasis on fresh fish, Kentish lamb, poultry and game in season. A two course businessman's lunch is available at £7.95, with a third course included for £9.50, and The George also has a comprehensive range of banqueting options and buffet menus, with vegetarian options not overlooked. All the leading credit cards are welcomed.

—————— • The George Hotel • ——————
High St, Rye
Tel: (0797) 222114

The Saltings Hotel Ltd.
&
The Old School Restaurant

HILDERS CLIFF
RYE EAST SUSSEX
TN31 7LD
TEL: RYE (0797) 223838

THE SALTINGS HOTEL and Old School Restaurant

Hilders Cliff, Rye.
Tel: (0797) 223838

Hours: *Open for coffee, lunch and dinner. Afternoon tea in summer.*

Average Prices: *A la Carte £11; Sun lunch £7.50; bar meals from £1.75.*

Wines: *From £5.25 per bottle.*

Refurbished from top to bottom and as pretty as a picture postcard, The Saltings is part of the charm of Rye. Enjoying spectacular views, the hotel is a haven of comfort and hospitality, with 15 bedrooms, all en suite and with the latest amenities, and a functions room which can cater for up to 75 guests. The Old School House Restaurant seats over 30, and here fish dishes are one of the specialities. Grilled whole Rye Bay plaice and sautéed king scallops are among the most popular. Other specialities are the tournedos Henry VIII, pork loin steaks 'Saltings', lamb cutlets dijonnaise and entrecôte steak Diane, and there are popular mixed grills, prime steaks and imaginative poultry dishes, such as supreme of chicken marechale and sautéed chicken hongroise (cooked in white wine with paprika and cream sauce). Vegetarians are well looked after and a bar snack menu is served at lunchtime. Access and Visa cards are welcomed and a car park is available at the rear of the hotel.

TOFFS

36–38 Cinque Ports Street, Rye. Tel: (0797) 222262

Hours:　　　　　*Open for lunch, 12–2.15pm, and dinner, 6–11pm, 7 days.*
Average Prices:　*A la Carte £10; Sun lunch £7.50 (3 courses).*
Wines:　　　　　*From £5.50 per bottle.*

"A totally new experience in eating out" is the preamble to the menu at this recent addition to Rye's choice of restaurants. An ambience of the 1920's prevails, with cane furniture, punkah fans, art deco décor, compatible soft furnishings and a white baby-grand piano. a large cocktail bar invites patrons to ponder their menu over a Tequila Sunrise or a Champagne Sidecar, to name but two from a long list. The menu has starters such as corn-on-the-cob, pâté, whitebait and Toffs' mushrooms, whilst the main courses take in char-grilled steaks, kebabs, fresh fish, pasta dishes, pizzas and vegetarian selections. There are also the chef's weekly specials to consider. The 80 cover dining area, being spacious and well ventilated, contains a raised balcony as an added feature. Depsite being elegant and sophisticated, this is a family restaurant (children are welcome), with prices to suit all pockets. Its atmosphere is also ideally suited to party functions, particularly with the pianist in attendance. All major credit cards are accepted.

36/38 Cinque Port Street, Rye.　　　　　　　　　　Tel: (0797) 222262

THE YPRES CASTLE INN

Gun Gardens, Church Square, Rye.
Tel: (0797) 223248

Hours: *Open for lunch and dinner.*
Average Prices: £3–£9.50.
Wines: *From £5.30 per bottle.*

Steeped in history, this hospitable inn is one of those rare establishments which prompts you to say "let's go and have a drink at Dick's". The landlord knows everyone; he remembers your face and is one of Rye's great characters. He's the Honorary Secretary of the RNLI and Dick's wife, Babs, has a selection of lifeboat souvenirs for sale at the inn. The Ypres Castle, affectionately known as 'The Wipers', is, therefore, a fun place, offering spectacular views over the harbour and fishing fleet, almost across to France. Live music is a further attraction and so is the food, with fresh fish to the fore. There's a home-made clam chowder, fillet and sirloins from the local butcher and traditional gammon steaks. The house speciality is mussels in Muscadet, served with garlic bread, and the bouillabaisse is always a favourite. Real ales are on draught and unusually there are no jukeboxes or bandits to disturb the atmosphere. The Wipers stands in the shadow of the Castle, now the town museum. It can also be reached up the steps from Fishmarket Road.

THE YPRES CASTLE INN

Gun Gardens, Rye
Tel: (0797) 223248

LANDGATE BISTRO

Landgate, Rye.
Tel: (0797) 222829

Hours: *Open for dinner, Tues–Sat (last orders 9.30pm).*
Average Prices: *A la Carte from £15.50.*
Wines: *From £5.50 per bottle.*

Nick Parkin's widely acknowledged restaurant has now won many accolades and has to be one of the most popular places in which to eat in the Rye area. There is always fresh Rye Bay fish, but the menu is both original and interesting. The monkfish with orange and vermouth sauce exemplifies the imagination, as does one of the specialities of the house, fresh scallop mousse with sauce beurre blanc. Alternatively, guests can choose from jugged hare, roast wild duck (with a port and orange sauce), potted quail or fresh kidneys sautéed with mushrooms, brandy and cream, and many other thoughtfully prepared dishes, all efficiently served. Children's helpings are available and a comprehensive, well-selected and realistically priced wine list accompanies. It is worth bearing in mind that this is an immensely popular little restaurant where booking in advance is not just strongly recommended but essential. There's no lunch, but dinner is served from 7pm. All the leading credit cards are welcomed: Access, Visa, American Express and Diner's Club.

THE HOPE ANCHOR HOTEL

Watchbell Street, Rye.
Tel: (0797) 222216

Hours:	*Open for coffee, lunch and dinner.*
Average Prices:	*A la Carte £10.50; Sun lunch £5.50 (2 courses).*
Wines:	*From £5 per bottle.*

This pretty 17th century hotel stands at Rye's highest easterly point and commands spectacular views across Strand Quay and Rye Harbour over to Hastings. Standing in Watchbell Street, named after the great bell which hung in the watch tower and rung in times of danger, this 15-bedroomed hotel is under the personal supervision of owners Lena and Derrick Baldock. From bar meals and snacks like home-cooked ham, fresh dressed crab and prawn salads to main menu à la carte selections such as fillet steak stuffed with oysters, honeyed duck with cloves, beef Stroganoff and rainbow trout, there is plenty to choose from. Fresh fish is plentiful, a house speciality being the seafood collation, consisting of scallops, prawns and scampi with smokey bacon and shallots, finished in a light cream sauce. Another favourite is the mixed fish livornaise (fish and shellfish with onions, tomatoes and garlic) and Sunday lunch is always popular, featuring a traditional English roast with a choice of vegetables. A friendly, relaxed atmosphere prevails throughout; a most welcoming hotel.

The Hope Anchor Hotel

Watchbell Street, Rye, East Sussex. Tel: (0797) 222216

THE QUEEN'S HEAD INN

Landgate, Rye. Tel: (0797) 222181
Hours: *Open for coffee, lunch and dinner (last orders 9.30pm).*
Average Prices: *A la Carte £7.50–£10; bar meals from £2.*
Wines: *From £5 per bottle.*

A coastal town hotel in the old style — and there aren't many left — where courtesy, care and personal attention to the needs of guests and visitors are as important as keeping the regulars happy, The Queen's Head is run by Peter and Jan Benn and chef, William. Both Peter and William were formerly chefs at London's famed Savoy and their reputation for food is second to none in the area. Fresh fish is the speciality, most of which is bought daily from Rye's fleet of fishing trawlers, and a range of pot meals has also become a great favourite, extending from a simple bowl of home-made soup with a baguette to steak and kidney pie with a puff pastry lid. There are also tagliatelle alla Roma, chilli con carne, lasagne verdi and a minced lamb hot pot, with vegetables, a layer of potatoes and then cheese. Steaks are highlighted by the 16oz T-bone, salads abound and, new and different are the American-style deli-sandwiches. There are eight to choose from, including hot pastrami on rye and Scottish smoked salmon. This inventive food at sensible prices is complemented by real ales and comfortable and reasonable accommodation. A function room is available for private parties, etc., and Access and Visa cards are accepted.

The Queen's Head, Landgate, Rye. Tel: (0797) 222181

THE GREEN OWL HOTEL

Old Lydd Road, Camber Sands, near Rye.
Tel: (0797) 225284

Hours: *Open for coffee, lunch and dinner, except Mon evenings (last orders 9.30pm).*

Average Prices: *A la Carte £4.50–£9.50; bar meals from £1.*

Wines: *House wines from £4.50 per bottle.*

This neat little hotel sits right against the dunes, on the other side of which are the famed Camber Sands, one of the finest and safest bathing beaches in the entire country. The Green Owl has six bedrooms (three en suite, three with shower and vanity unit), as well as a small letting bungalow. Its location makes it convenient for Rye and Romney Marsh, and for activities such as bird watching at nearby reserves, golf, riding, fishing and watersports. The food is all home-cooked and has a good reputation. Bar meals usually feature fresh fish from Rye Bay and various chip meals — sausages, pasties, chicken nuggets, etc. The à la carte selection is modestly priced and includes the fillet, sirloin, rump and T-bone steaks for which The Green Owl is well known, as well as gammon, grilled trout, chicken and fillets of plaice. For a snack there are brown or white rolls with a choice of fillings, sandwiches, salads and ploughman's lunches. White house wines range from dry to sweet and there is also a house claret. Real ales are on draught. Children welcome. Car park.

The Green Owl Hotel
Camber Sands
Nr. Rye.
Tel: 0797
225 284

THE FLACKLEY ASH HOTEL AND RESTAURANT

Peasmarsh, near Rye.
Tel: (079 721) 651

Hours: *Open for dinner and lunchtime and evening bar meals.*
Average Prices: *A la Carte £13–£17; bar meals from £2.50.*
Wines: *From £6.50 per bottle.*

Just a few miles from the centre of Rye, in the village of Peasmarsh, is one of the most welcoming country house hotels in the South East. The Flackley Ash Hotel and Restaurant has a fine reputation for food and luxurious accommodation (30 en suite bedrooms, with every amenity). There is a leisure club (complete with heated pool, sauna and gymnasium) and full banqueting facilities, catering for up to 100 guests. Bar meals feature fresh fish; indeed the hotel has its own fishing trawler. As a result, Rye Bay plaice, dabs and sole are always on the menu, along with home-cooked ham, scampi, gammon steaks, stuffed mussels, salads, deep-fried mushrooms and more. Bar meals continue in the evenings and dinner is also served à la carte in the restaurant. Steaks are prominent, so is seafood, and there are curries and other chef's creations which vary with the seasons and weather. To accompany, there is a comprehensive wine list and a choice of six house wines. The Flackley Ash Hotel is an ideal base for exploring this interesting corner of Sussex and Kent, and accepts all leading credit cards.

Best Western

Telephone:
Peasmarsh (079-721)
651

Clive & Jeanie Bennett
welcome you to the

FLACKLEY ASH
HOTEL & RESTAURANT

THE ROSE AND CROWN

Northiam Road, Beckley.
Tel: (079 74) 2161

Hours: *Open for coffee, lunch and dinner.*
Average Prices: *A la Carte from £7.50; bar meals from £1.50.*
Wines: *From £5 per bottle.*

This fine inn is now family-owned, a free house and a rising star amongst Sussex's country inns. Pretty, spacious and airy, the two adjoining bars are cooled by overhead fans and the clean cool décor is soft on the eye and pleasantly refreshing. There is a separate restaurant, seating 22, and bar meals are available in both bars. A blackboard shows the daily special, which may range from home-made steak and kidney pie to lasagne, scampi or chicken curry. The evening menu offers some eight starters, typical examples being melon with port, avocado with prawns, toast with pâté, smoked salmon with brown bread, and whitebait. Main course selections include trout with almonds, sirloin and fillet steaks, steak au poivre, beef bourguignon, chicken chasseur and more. The prominent desserts feature home-made apple pie with fresh cream, coconut fudge, cheesecake, banana split and Alabama soft rock pie — just a few from the wide and frequently changing range of puddings. The Rose and Crown, run by Bob, Val, Karen and Sean is a friendly place, with a pleasant atmosphere, real log fires in winter and real ales on draught.

The Rose and Crown, Northiam Road, Beckley. Tel (079 74) 2161

THE CROWN AND THISTLE

Main Road, Northiam. Tel: (079 74) 3224

Hours: *Open for coffee, lunch and dinner (last orders 10pm).*
No meals Sun evening.

Average Prices: *A la Carte £11; bar meals from £1.*

Wines: *From £4.25 per bottle.*

This attractive old inn is set right in the village of Northiam and dates from the 15th century when it was, originally, a farmhouse. Very much a centre of village activity, it retains the village pub atmosphere in its traditional public and saloon bars and has a separate restaurant seating up to 20. A pleasant garden and a large car park are further attributes. Brian and Carole-Anne Wooding personally supervise all the activities of the inn. The à la carte selection has starters such as fresh dressed Cromer crab, served in the shell; asparagus parcel with hot butter sauce; seafood crêpe and prawn cocktail. Main courses feature Crown and Thistle sole with prawns, cream and brandy; royal lamb with redcurrant and lemon; grilled salmon steaks and fillet or rump steaks with all the trimmings. All vegetables are fresh and organically grown and to finish there are profiteroles, hot cherry crêpes and ice cream. At lunchtime the specials range from a popular fisherman's pie to lasagne verdi and Lancashire hot pot. Oak beams and log fires set the scene and there is a functions room for up to 100 guests. Booking in advance is advisable for weekends.

The Crown & Thistle

Main Road
Northiam
Tel: (079 74) 3224

THE ROTHER VALLEY INN

Station Road, Northiam.
Tel: (079 74) 2116

Hours: *Open for lunch, dinner and bar meals (last orders 10pm).*

Average Prices: A la Carte £8.50–£12; bar meals from £1.10.

Wines: *From £4.50 per bottle.*

One of the most popular inns in this part of the county, The Rother Valley has fine accommodation and an informal and friendly atmosphere. There's always something going on; the inn has live music from time to time and it adjoins the steam railway station which opens in spring 1990 as part of the Kent and East Sussex Railway. The restaurant menu here offers great variety. There's a good selection of starters, ranging from frog's legs sautéed in garlic butter and escargots bourguignon to garlic mushrooms and melon and prawn salad. Everything is home-made and the chicken in cream and mushroom sauce is one of the favourite main courses. Lamb Shrewsbury (lamb in a port sauce), gammon provençale and pork au raisins (flambéed in calvados and finished with cream) are other choices, or there are shark steaks, poached salmon trout, veal Mornay, venison with a pepper sauce and roast duck à l'orange. Steak lovers will find a choice of five, including steak au poivre and T-bone.

Rother Valley Inn, Station Rd, Northiam. Tel: (079 74) 2116

THE KING'S HEAD INN

Udimore, near Rye. Tel: (0424) 882349

Hours: *Open for coffee, lunch and dinner (last orders 9.30pm). Afternoon teas in summer. No food Mon in winter.*

Average Prices: *A la Carte £8.50; bar meals from £1.*

Wines: *From £4 per bottle.*

This fine old inn dates from about 1750 and stands high on the ridge which gives the best of all views over marsh and meadow to Winchelsea Beach. With its polished oak bar, dark beams and open fires in winter, The King's Head is an old favourite which has been given new life. Anita and Trevor Jones moved in at the beginning of 1989 and have transformed every aspect. From a kitchen supervised by a dietician, no less, emerge home-cooked soups and pâtés to start,followed by main dishes of steak braised in Guinness and a special steak and kidney pie with real ale. The lasagne and spaghetti bolognaise are prepared with fresh herbs (some imported from Italy) and the difference is there to be tasted. Fish comes fresh each day from Rye, the gammon is home-cured and the coq au vin consists of an entire half-chicken per person. Popular desserts include rice pudding, apple pie made with fresh Bramleys, and an all-fresh fruit salad. This is a real pub specialising in food and not a restaurant disguised as a pub. Real ales on draught. Children's room.

The King's Head Inn

Udimore, near Rye, East Sussex

THE HAMMONDS COUNTRY HOTEL

Udimore, near Rye. Tel: (0797) 225020

Hours:	*Open for lunch, Tues–Sun, and dinner, Thurs–Sat, for non-residents. Cream teas Sat/Sun in summer.*
Average Prices:	*A la Carte from £8.50; Sun lunch from £4.50 (2 courses).*
Wines:	*From £4.95 per bottle.*

A mere description of the views from this exquisite country house hotel could not possibly do the subject justice. The hotel itself, a Queen Anne period building, is set in ten acres of gardens and woodland, has ten luxurious bedrooms (five en suite) and a mini golf course, tennis courts and a heated outdoor pool. Such peace and tranquillity is conducive to a healthy appetite and The Hammonds aims to satisfy this with, amongst other dishes, fish fresh from the Rye fishing boats. There's lamb from the Romney Marshes (reputedly the best in the world) and local fruit and vegetables. The menu changes regularly and with the seasons, mixing traditional British fare with Continental favourites. Lamb cutlets may be served with reform sauce or there may be escalope of veal Holstein. Desserts are homely and range from old recipes for suet pudding to fresh apple crumble. Many people's first choice to 'get away from it all', The Hammonds is situated five minutes from Rye on the B2089. Access and Visa cards welcomed.

UDIMORE, NR. RYE, EAST SUSSEX TN31 6AJ
TELEPHONE: (0797) 223167/225020

THE FAMOUS SEVEN STARS INN
and Captain's Table Restaurant

High Street, Robertsbridge. Tel: (0580) 880333

Hours: *Open for coffee, lunch and dinner, except Sun evening (last orders 9pm, 9.30pm Fri/Sat).*

Average Prices: *A la Carte £10; Sun lunch £6.75 (4 courses).*

Wines: *From £5.50 per bottle (white); £6.50 per bottle (red).*

Dating from around 1380, The Famous Seven Stars Inn, with its Captain's Table Restaurant, is the oldest pub in Sussex and is most definitely haunted! The ghost is that of a monk, dressed in a red habit, and has been mentioned in many books about the supernatural. The building itself has a faithfully recorded history dating back to 1194. A fascinating and delightful inn, the bar meals here include a range of ploughman's lunches and other home-made specialities, whilst the Captain's Table Restaurant, which is separate from the main bar, specialises in steak and fish dishes. Starters include langoustines in garlic butter, whitebait, pâté, smoked salmon, local smoked trout and, most popular, prawn cocktail with Marie Rose sauce. Main courses feature fresh Dover sole, Scottish wild salmon, Darwell local trout and seafood salads. Steaks are from prime beef (a choice of different weights) and include steak Diane, steak au poivre, mustard and country-style. Fine home-made desserts and a good range of wines and real ales are available too. Children are welcome.

The Famous Seven Stars Inn & Captain's Table

High Street, Robertsbridge. Tel: (0580) 880333

THE GEORGE INN

High Street, Robertsbridge. Tel: (0580) 880315

Hours: *Open for coffee, lunch and dinner (last orders 10.45pm). Afternoon tea in summer.*

Average Prices: *A la Carte £12–£15; Sun lunch £4.50; bar meals from £1.50.*

Wines: *From £5 per bottle.*

Novelist-poet Hilaire Belloc was frequently a guest at Robertsbridge's George Inn and wrote some of the early chapters of his book *Four Men* whilst staying here. The book begins: "Nine years ago, when I was sitting in The George at Robertsbridge, drinking that port of theirs and staring into the fire . . .". It's changed, of course. Now there are delightful landscaped gardens with ponds and a waterfall, a barbecue area, amusements and a large car park. There is a 30-seat restaurant, a functions room for 50 and four letting rooms. Snacks are shown daily on the blackboard, with sandwiches, ploughman's lunches, salads and basket meals. The dinner menu has a French accent, offering snails, king prawns in butter with garlic and bisque d'homard amongst the starters, and sole bonne femme, chateaubriand and chicken Kiev as examples of main courses. Owners Ken and Marion Woodhams have aimed for a 'country manor' feel and part of the main bar/reception space is designed as a manorial drawing room. All major credit cards are welcome, as are children, who have a half-price menu.

The George Inn High Street Robertsbridge

Telephone: (0580) 880315

143

JACK FULLER'S

NEAR BRIGHTLING
EAST SUSSEX
TN32 5HD

TELEPHONE (042 482) 212

JACK FULLER'S

Near Brightling. Tel: (042 482) 212

Hours:	*Open for lunch 12–3pm and dinner 7–11pm. (Last orders 10pm). No meals Mon.*
Average Prices:	*Lunch £3.50–£8; dinner £4.50–£10.*
Wines:	*From £5 per bottle.*

The accolades of two major food guides have literally put Brightling, in East Sussex, on the map. Extolled by Egon Ronay as "one of the really top food pubs", Jack Fuller's is a Sussex beauty spot in which to enjoy some of the best food the county has to offer.

Owners Roger Berman and Shirl Telfer plan to develop their concept of English rural foods over the next few years. The gigantic menu is entirely produced on the premises, with fresh produce brought in each day. Puddings and pies are exceptional favourites; try the gammon and onion pudding or the prawn and halibut pie. Beef stew with dumplings can be served with a cheesy leek and potato bake, and another unusual vegetable side dish is the Stilton cauliflower. Indeed, imagination for a change has inspired some exciting vegetarian dishes, including cashew and aubergine bake, and a vegetarian spotted dick for dessert. But probably the highlight of the menu is the steak and kidney pudding.

Desserts are another great attraction, with blackcurrant and apple crumble, sticky treacle tart, Mother's bread pudding and chocolate whisky charlotte. English cheeses abound in the selection.

Dishes of the day are also offered, with fresh crab, lobster and salmon, as well as curries and many, many salads.

Jack Fuller's also has a fine reputation for its stock of English wines. The wine list boasts the largest range in England, majoring on famous vineyards such as Penshurst and Lamberhurst. Apple and organic wines produced locally are also listed. Imported wines are also available, from all over the world and the list has a particularly good mid-range selection. Fresh orange juice is squeezed daily. Cask-conditioned ales and ciders are always on offer.

'Mad' Jack Fuller, a late 18th and early 19th century MP, was a wealthy eccentric who became famous for his follies, which can be seen in and around Brightling. For each folly there is at least one story handed down as to why it was built. It was at one time believed that, on his death in 1834, he was interred within the 25ft high pyramid which is his monument in Brightling churchyard, supposedly buried seated at an iron table, a full meal spread before him, a bottle of claret at arm's length, dressed for dinner and wearing a top hat!

Jack Fuller's has a lovely garden, a raised terrace with tables and umbrellas, and a spacious car park. Despite the fact that over 70 can be seated, it is always advisable to reserve a table at weekends.

THE CASTLE INN

Bodiam.
Tel: (058 083) 330

Hours: *Open for lunch and dinner, except Sun/Mon evenings. Bar meals every day.*

Average Prices: *A la Carte from £6.50; bar meals from £1.*

Wines: *From £4.50 per bottle; £1 per glass.*

Unspoilt, and typical of an English rural inn, the famous Castle Inn at Bodiam is always attractive. In the shadow of historic Bodiam Castle, the inn has a fine reputation for food, both in the bar and in the 34-seat restaurant, and is run with pride by owners Candy and John Barnett and Anthony Webb. Dishes of the day are chalked up on the blackboard — an indication of the freshness of the fare — and may include fresh fish from the coast, locally caught trout or the home-made steak and kidney pie. The à la carte selection offers great variety, from steaks to salmon and from pheasant to venison, and there is, in addition, a set price autumn and winter menu at under £10 for three courses plus fresh coffee. Weather permitting, there are outdoor barbecues on Sunday evenings in summer, and special supper menus change with the seasons too. For those tempted to stay longer, very reasonably priced accommodation is available, inclusive of a hearty full English breakfast. A function room caters for up to 120 guests and, in the bar, real ales are on draught.

The Castle

FREE HOUSE WITH RESTAURANT

BODIAM
Near Robertsbridge, East Sussex
Tel: Staplecross 0580-83330

THE HARRIER INN

Link Hill, Sandhurst.
Tel: (0580) 850323

Hours: Open 11am–11pm for coffee, lunch and dinner (last orders 9.30pm). No meals Tues evening.

Average Prices: £1–£10.

Wines: From £4.75 per bottle.

The Harrier Inn is an unspoilt free house on the Kent-Sussex border, on the road between Sandhurst and Northiam. A fine, traditional, English country inn which specialises in serving home-cooked fresh food, this is an extremely popular rendezvous for visitors and tourists as well as the regulars. The cold cabinet serves locally-cured ham, dressed crab and similar dishes with a variety of salads, dressings and crusty bread. The steak and kidney pie with a crispy pastry topping is different in that it is made with Guinness, and then there is chicken Kiev or lasagne, shell-on prawns and fish, fresh daily from Rye Bay, cooked to order and always a major attraction. Smoked chicken breast and mackerel are also available, and the steaks are well-hung for tenderness. Real ales are on draught at the bar, and the attractive garden and pleasant atmosphere make The Harrier a local favourite. Debbie and Roger King are the welcoming hosts. With these realistic prices, credit cards are not accepted.

THE HARRIER INN

LINK HILL
SANDHURST
KENT

Hosts: Roger and Debbie

TEL (0580) 850323

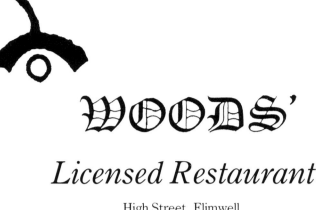

WOODS'

Licensed Restaurant

High Street, Flimwell,
Wadhurst, East Sussex.
Telephone: Flimwell (058087) 342

Hours: *Open for dinner, Tues–Sat from 7.30pm (last orders 10pm). Sun lunch 12–2pm.*

Average Prices: *A la Carte £12.95.*

Wines: *From £5.75 per bottle.*

Between the A21 Flimwell traffic lights and the road into Ticehurst, this pleasant little restaurant can be found, tucked away in a peaceful country setting. Menus change regularly, but the following provide some examples of dishes available from time to time. French onion soup, escargots in the shell with garlic butter, baked crab claws with a mild mustard sauce, Portuguese mussels in olive oil with garlic and white wine, shellfish Mornay and grapefruit and apple cocktail are all popular starters. For main course there may be pork calvados or an unusual salmis of wood pigeon, braised in a claret sauce with red cabbage and almonds. Woods' recipe for chicken is to cook it in strips with mushrooms and cream, lemon and parsley, and their baked trout is wrapped in filo pastry. Fillet steak with onions, mushrooms and oysters is another possibility, as is the supreme of beef with fresh horseradish and cream, fried in butter. Coffee and petits fours follow the dessert or cheeseboard choice.

Index

ALPHABETICAL INDEX TO ESTABLISHMENTS

ALPHABETICAL INDEX TO TOWNS AND VILLAGES